Day Skipper Motor Cruising

Denise Bréhaut
and
Paul Hay

Helmsman Books

D1382535

First Published in 1997 by
The Crowood Press Ltd
Ramsbury, Marlborough
Wiltshire SN8 2HR

www.crowood.com

This impression 2002

British Library Cataloguing in Publication Data

A catalogue record for this book is available from the British Library.

ISBN 1 85223 853 4

Picture Credits
Photographs by Denise Bréhaut
Line-drawings by Andrew Creen

Dedication
To Stan Bréhaut without whose skills *Sarpedon* would not be the vessel she is and
whose support as a 'human answer phone' has allowed Prestige Power to continue
and thrive.

Acknowlegments
We would like to thank Gill Norton and Marion Bréhaut. for their help, support and
encouragement given whilst writing this book. Our thanks also go to Jason Watling
of Land & Marine Products Ltd, Bordon, Hants, for demonstrating thé Jason's Cradle
recovery device.

Tidal Stream extracts on pages 48, 50 and 51 are derived from Admiralty material by
permission of the Controller of Her Majesty's Stationery Office and the UK
Hydrographic Office.

Typeset by Multimedia Works Ltd, Gloucester
Printed and bound in Great Britain by The Cromwell Press Ltd, Trowbridge, Wiltshire

CONTENTS

INTRODUCTION

The aim of this book is to cover the syllabuses for RYA Helmsman and Day Skipper practical motor cruising courses. This would be a six-day practical course for anyone with no previous practical experience. It assumes theoretical knowledge equivalent to the Day Skipper theory course, which would be conducted prior to the Day Skipper practical course. We have tried to revise this theoretical information within the text wherever possible.

The Day Skipper practical course itself is conducted in four days if the student already has boat handling skills. Courses may be conducted on an RYA recognized school boat, or on your own vessel. The aim of the Day Skipper practical course is to teach pilotage, navigation, seamanship and boat handling. The standard is that required to skipper a motor cruiser safely by day in waters with which the student is familiar.

Motor Boats v. Yachts

People choose power over sail for many reasons. Some like the exhilaration of speed, some just have a shortage of time, others, in their later years, find the power-driven vessel easier to run. There is a definite comfort in a motor boat which is seldom found in a yacht of comparable size. It is impractical to have carpeted floors when you are going to throw wet sails on to them, and constant hot water for showers and domestic use would be very heavy on power consumption. Many of these niceties come as standard on most motor cruisers. It is very pleasant to step out of your bunk on to deep-pile carpet and into a hot shower. If you work full time and only have the weekends free, you can visit France from the South Coast, enjoy a good meal and still get some sleep! To do this on a yacht could mean sailing all night. On the down side is the cost of fuel and constant noise from the engines, which does not compare favourably with the tranquillity of sailing by the wind, which of course is free!

The high topsides of a motor boat allow for plenty of accommodation inside. However, there is a price to pay for this when it comes to slow speed boat handling in anything more than light airs. With a planing hull, there is a high proportion of the vessel out of the water, allowing the boat to be pushed around by the wind. Displacement vessels will be less affected in this way. On the whole, motor boats are much more difficult to handle in harbour than sailing yachts.

They do have throttles and a steering wheel, but that is where the similarity to your car ends. Anyone who has tried to squeeze twelve metres of luxurious high-powered pride and joy into the average marina berth, in an exceptionally variable force 6 wind, will testify to the difficulties! There are, of course, techniques to help overcome these problems, which will be covered in this book.

If the weather changes quickly there is a chance of outrunning it in a motor boat. If you are caught out, however, you are down to sailing speeds and planing hulls are nothing like as stable as sailing yachts in rough conditions. If your choice of vessel is a heavy displacement boat, you will be less troubled by bad weather.

Cost is another important consideration. You will pay more for a metre of motor boat than for a metre of sailing yacht and as already mentioned, they are more expensive to run.

We guess that, if you have gone as far as buying this book, power is your preference. Our advice to you is to learn how to handle your craft and enjoy it. Close-quarters handling of both yachts and power craft must be one of the most neglected areas of practical boating. Yet, when done neatly and without fuss, it can generate feelings of immense satisfaction and contribute greatly to your boating pleasure. The tragedy of the 'just like driving a car' syndrome, is that it leads to so many boats, more especially motor boats, being abandoned by their owners after only a few disastrous outings, simply because they have ended in embarrassment or minor damage.

Good boat handling is a skill that anyone can learn with a little bit of guidance and plenty of practice. So don't leave your pride and joy sitting in the marina next season. Find out how it's done properly and safely and give yourself some practice in a quiet backwater beyond the gaze of smug faces. When you feel confident, go out and discover a level of enjoyment in your boating that you and your crew will relish.

1

HULL FORMS AND

PROPULSION SYSTEMS

In this chapter we will briefly discuss the types of motor boat which are commonly available. There are many and various craft on the market and if you are not careful, the first one you buy could be the wrong one. Not because there is anything wrong with the vessel itself, but because it does not suit the use for which you have bought it. If at all possible, it is better to try to spend a few days on a selection of boats before you make your final choice. There are three basic hull types to consider: displacement, semi-displacement and planing.

Types of Hull

Displacement

When under way, displacement hulls displace their own weight in the water. That is, they will make a hole in the water equal to their own weight, which has to be continually generated by pushing that amount of water out of the way as the vessel moves along. This motion will set up a transverse wave pattern which limits the vessel's maximum economical speed (see Fig 1). The faster you push the boat

Displacement hull showing transverse wave.

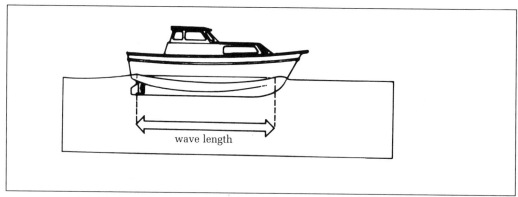

Fig 1   Transverse wave.

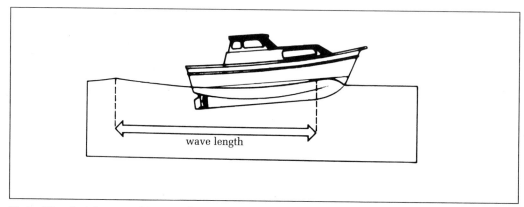

Fig 2   Wave length as speed increased.

through the water, the greater the wave-length will become. As wavelength increases, the second wave or stern wave will move along the vessel eventually falling behind the boat, leaving the stern unsupported. The boat is then left climbing uphill on the side of a bow wave which it has itself created. Its stern will have sunk into a trough, at an attitude which is both uncomfortable and expensive in fuel (see Fig 2). The transverse wave is not a function of the size of the vessel, but the speed. The longer the hull, the greater the speed achieved before this restriction is reached. For the mathematicians, the formula for calculating maximum displacement speed is: V in knots = 1.35 $\sqrt{\text{LWL}}$ in feet. Examples of this type of craft are Pedro and Grandbanks.

Planing

Planing boats overcome the above limitation by a combination of engine power and hull form, which enables them to lift partially clear of the water. This reduces the resistance because there is less water to move and enables the boat to go faster than its displacement speed, without an excessive increase in power. For maximum lift and ease of planing a flat bottom would be best. However, in any sort of sea this shape would slam intolerably and directional stability would be poor. A Deep V-shaped hull can cut through waves and is good for sea keeping, but needs higher speed to plane. It is best to compromise this V shape with a flat aft section for high lift where the weight is.

A wide beam is best to take a vessel from maximum displacement to planing speed, which commonly occurs in the region of ten knots. Once on the plane, however, the narrower the beam the better, as this will produce less friction. A Deep V hull with a large beam and spray rails is the best compromise. The spray rails effectively reduce the beam as the speed increases (see Fig 3). The disadvantage is that these hulls will lack directional stability at low speeds. This makes them the poorer choice for inland waterways or at sea in very rough conditions, when speed must be reduced causing the vessel to come off the plane. Examples of this type of craft are Birchwood, Princess, Fairline and Sunseeker.

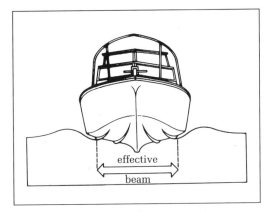

Fig 3   Spray rails reduce beam as speed increases.

Semi-Displacement

Semi-displacement craft combine the characteristics of both displacement and planing hulls. A round bilge with a keel and flattish aft section is not as efficient as a true planing hull when planing, or as a displacement hull at displacement speeds. However, they do lack the vices of the specialist craft and can give acceptably high speeds while still retaining good sea-keeping qualities. Examples of these are Nelson, Weymouth and Hardy.

Engines and Drive Units

Outboard

A vessel up to six metres in length could have a single outboard engine, with larger vessels probably having twin engines. Having said that, two engines are always better than one, for safety reasons, regardless of how small the vessel is. Outboards are usually used on small vessels, though they are available up to

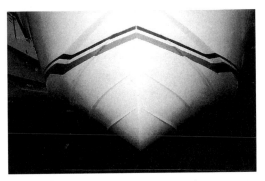

Spray rails reduce beam width as speed increases.

Single engine with large rudder and skeg protection.

Outdrive units may be inspected while in the water.

300hp these days. Larger outboards will have 'power tilt' for trimming.

Inboard

Again, inboard installations may either be single or twin engines. A single engine will usually have a large rudder for effective slow speed handling and skeg protection for the propeller. Twin engines will be mounted side by side and the propeller shafts supported by 'P' or 'A' brackets. Planing or semi-displacement craft have small rudders to reduce drag at higher speeds, which means they are less effective for slow speed manoeuvring.

Outdrive Unit

Outdrive units are typically found on vessels up to forty feet and usually on planing boats. Once again, they may be single or twin units. They are easier and cheaper to install than shaft drive systems. The engine itself is mounted inboard and the outdrive leg fitted on the back of the boat. This removes the necessity to produce expensive tunnel

mouldings for propeller shafts. The outdrive leg can be raised for inspection, if you suspect a fouled propeller for example. It can also be raised when in shallow water or when drying out. This form of propulsion gives high manoeuvrability at low speeds, but only when power is applied. The outdrive leg can be tilted for trimming.

Trimming

The trim of a vessel refers to the angle between the fore and aft centre line of the boat and the horizontal. It may also refer to the athwartship angle of the vessel in the water, i.e. listing to port or starboard. All vessels are carefully designed with trim in mind, when it comes to the positioning of engines, fuel tanks and other weighty objects. However, the designers cannot take into account every variation of speed, wind and sea condition. The trim will also alter depending on whether you have your fuel and water tanks empty or full. Variable trim is required to alter the attitude of the vessel for head seas

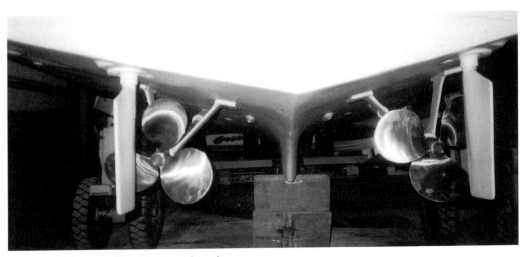

Planing craft have small rudders to reduce drag.

and stern seas. Three to five degrees bows up is the usual running angle.

Trim Tabs

We have seen that as a hull exceeds its displacement speed and before it starts to plane, it assumes an exaggerated bows up attitude. Trim tabs should be fully down during the transition to planing speeds. This generates more lift on the stern and reduces the tendency to assume an exaggerated bows up attitude. It also enables the boat to get on to the plane at a lower speed and with less expenditure of power. If you are using an outdrive leg, then trim it fully 'in'. This will give further lift to the stern. As speed increases on the plane the hull starts to assume a bows down attitude, because the trim tabs will now be providing too much lift. Gently easing up the trim tabs will reduce the lift on the stern and allow the bows to rise. This maintains the correct trim by reducing the wetted surface of the hull and therefore reducing the drag.

Power Trim and Tilt

On most large outboards and all outdrive units a mechanism exists for altering the angle of the outboard or outdrive leg. The leg itself can be tilted both positively and negatively, by means of a servo motor mechanism driving a small hydraulic ram. This has the effect of altering the horizontal thrust line of the propeller. **Power Trim** is the term given to small movements of the leg, usually in the range of + and − 5 to 7 degrees. These movements are made with engine power on, to affect the running angle of the boat. **Power Tilt** is a large positive movement of the leg up to 45 degrees, which can be used for inspection purposes or when beaching the boat. This must only be done with the engines stopped. Putting the engines into neutral is not sufficient.

Generally speaking, you should use trim tabs and power trim (−5 degrees) to get the vessel on to the plane. Then as speed increases, take off the trim tabs and use power trim for fine running adjustments. When the boat is up and running, it will assume a 3 to 5 degree bows up attitude. If the leg was not trimmed, it would in effect be pushing the boat out of the water. Trim the leg out to the +3 to 5 degrees running angle, so that the propeller thrust line remains parallel with the water. This ensures maximum efficiency, and therefore maximum speed.

To summarize then, once up and running on the plane, in smooth waters, set the engine revs and then adjust the trim tabs and power trim for maximum speed. Apply power trim in small amounts and wait for the effect to take place, before applying more. You should be able to achieve a "free knot" with good trimming.

Power tilt raises the legs up to 45 degrees for inspection and beaching. Most tilt/trim systems will have a cut-out and alarm which activates at about +5 degrees. To tilt the leg to greater angles, this cut-out must be overridden. It is imperative that the engines are stopped before the legs are tilted to angles of greater than +5 degrees, to prevent serious damage to the shaft couplings in the outdrive leg.

Summary

If possible, it is always better to spend time onboard the type of vessel you think you may want to purchase. Talk to as many people as you can for their opinions and advice. Generally speaking, shaft driven vessels tend to be easier to handle than those fitted with outdrives. Be clear what use you have in mind for your prospective vessel. There is little point in buying a fast planing boat if your intention is to keep it on a river with a six knot speed limit. If you intend to take off into the sunset and cruise around the world, you will probably require the range and sea keeping capabilities of a slower displacement vessel. If you plan to use the vessel for local family outings, the accommodation aspects could be of more importance to you. However, if you are short of time but would like to travel far afield, then the speed of the vessel is likely to be a priority. Have all these factors clear in your mind when you start looking around for a vessel to purchase. As you can see, criteria will vary dramatically according to the intended use.

Questions

1 Would you operate power tilt to 45 degrees with the engine in neutral?
2 Name the three basic hull types and engine configurations.
3 Why is it important to trim your vessel?

Answers

1 Never, as you can seriously damage the shaft couplings in the outdrive leg if the engine is not stopped.
2 Displacement, semi-displacement and planing. Outboard, outdrive and inboard.
3 To help the vessel get on to the plane, to trim the vessel for sea conditions and achieve maximum speed at minimum cost.

2

Introduction To The Boat and Preparation For Sea

A safety brief is a very important part of the introduction to a vessel. It can be divided into three areas: safety of you as an individual, the crew as a group and safety of the vessel itself. Safety equipment is only useful if it is properly maintained and your crew know where to find it and how to use it. There are also a number of checks to perform before you start your engines, which will be discussed at the end of this chapter.

Personal Safety

Life-Jackets

One life-jacket should be available for each person onboard. A life-jacket is intended to support a body in the water and maintain the mouth clear of the surface. If a casualty falls face down in the water, a life-jacket should be capable of turning him on to his back. They are not to be confused with buoyancy aids which are only intended to provide additional buoyancy. There are four types of life jacket available:

1   The solid type provides permanent buoyancy. These are bulky and therefore not suitable for continuous wear onboard.

2   The oral air inflation type requires the wearer to inflate the jacket by mouth. They have the advantage of being compact when stowed and are therefore suitable for continuous wear. Their main disadvantage is that they require the wearer to inflate them orally before they provide any buoyancy. This is satisfactory if the wearer is forewarned of the need for inflation. If, however, the casualty was suddenly immersed in water at British sea temperatures, oral inflation would be difficult and if he was unconscious the jacket would be of no use at all.

3   The manual gas inflation type requires the wearer to activate a gas cylinder, by pulling a toggle or squeezing a trigger. When this is done, just the correct amount of gas is released to inflate the jacket. As this happens, the poppers or velcro fastenings will be automatically released. This system removes the need for oral inflation but still does not assist the unconscious casualty.

4   The automatic gas inflation type requires no user input other than to be wearing the jacket. On immersion, the gas inflation system is automatically acti-vated to inflate the jacket. This type has the advantage of compactness and there-fore encourages continuous wear. It is effective for the unconscious or severely

gasping casualty. Most of these types are designed to be attached to foul-weather jackets and the top of the range type usually incorporate a safety harness system.

All the gas inflation type jackets will feature an oral air inflation tube should the gas system fail. However, it is essential that the gas system is tried first before resorting to oral inflation. Partially inflating the jacket with air followed by gas inflation is likely to result in an orange frill around your neck as the over-inflated lifejacket bursts!

Whichever type of life jacket you choose, it should be fitted with a whistle to attract attention (and keep up morale while you are waiting to be rescued), reflective tape, a light if you boat after dark and a small strap for lifting you out of the water.

Finally, as part of your safety brief,

Ensure that all persons onboard have access to a life-jacket and know how to wear it correctly.

ensure that all persons onboard know where the life-jackets are stowed, how to wear them correctly and how to inflate them if necessary. Because there are so many different designs of jacket, it can take a minute to fathom out how to fit an unfamiliar type. The time to be working this out is in harbour, not as the ship is going down.

WHEN ARE YOU GOING TO WEAR A LIFE-JACKET?

Some might choose to wear them all the time, others only when there is increased danger. Use during night cruising is essential and when making dinghy trips and cruising in fog. Any non-swimmers or children in your crew should wear them all the time. There is an increased risk of losing your grip and falling overboard in rough weather. What you consider to be rough weather is personal, and may differ from craft to craft. Always offer a life-jacket to people who come onboard, especially if they are not used to boats. They might be uncomfortable with the way the boat moves around and may be unsteady on their feet. Never make people feel embarrassed to wear one, there is nothing macho in drowning.

Safety Harnesses

Harnesses tend to be considered as a piece of safety equipment for the sailing yachtsman. He would have a harness as first choice, whereas you would go for a life-jacket. However, you should have at least one on a motor boat.

There are three types of harness. You can buy a stand-alone type which is worn on its own or underneath your life-jacket. Again, practise putting it on as they can be awkward to get into. The second type

A safety harness keeps you attached to the boat.

of harness is an integral part of your foul-weather jacket. The last option is the neatest one, when the harness is constructed as part of your life-jacket. The latter two options require an additional lifeline to attach you to the vessel. The gibb self-locking hook is considered by many to be the best choice. Jack stays are a useful inexpensive addition to your safety gear, again favoured more by the sailor. These can be a length of webbing along your side decks, to allow your crew to walk the entire length of the boat without unclipping.

WHEN ARE YOU GOING TO WEAR A HARNESS?

If you are travelling along at twenty knots, you probably would not want to be attached to the boat. Should you fall in, you would be brought up very hard,

dragged along, thrown against the side of the boat and even forcibly drowned before the helmsman had time to stop. It would be better to fall free in a life-jacket. However, if you need to send someone on to the foredeck in rough conditions, it would be better to have them attached to the boat. The person recovering a man overboard should wear a harness, as the last thing you want is a second person in the water. The boat will be sideways on to the wind and waves and this is its most unstable attitude. In really rough conditions you might want the harness clipped around the seat on the flybridge. Nobody chooses to be out in such extreme conditions, but it is always possible to be caught out by unexpected weather. Receiving a tow would be another occasion when it might be wise for the crew to be in a harness. Anyone who feels seasick and wishes to remain on deck should be attached. They will not be co-ordinated and could possibly be showing suicidal tendencies!

You should think twice about asking your crew to wear a harness in thick fog. The biggest danger is being run down by a large vessel which has not seen you on its radar. The vessel could come out of the gloom and cut your boat in half causing it to sink very quickly with crew still attached. This is one of the reasons why we try to get into shallow water on such occasions. However, as skipper you might make the decision that there is not a lot of shipping around and there is more danger of someone falling in and you losing sight of him in the fog.

Clothing

Your crew should have effective foul-weather jackets and trousers. Sea boots

Boating in the snow, when warm clothing is essential.

can be useful for rainy days. When it is rough you can get very wet on the flybridge. There is a tendency to think that because you are in a motor boat, as soon as the weather becomes a little unpleasant you will go inside. In fact, it is almost the reverse. The worse the weather gets, the more you would rather helm the boat from outside. When inside, the visibility can be hampered by large blind areas and sometimes tinted windows can hinder. There is also little feel for what is going on outside. As you become more experienced and venture on longer trips, you may choose to helm from inside once you are out in open water, with light traffic and less risk of flotsam and jetsam in the water.

Safety of the Crew

Lifebelt and Light

The action of the remaining crew, if someone falls in the water, should be included in your safety brief. Shout 'Man overboard' to warn everyone onboard that

someone is in the water. Grab the nearest lifebelt, which should be attached to a light and drogue. Throw the lifebelt in, even if you are 20–30 metres away from your man, because it marks the area. Watch and point. The sea looks the same wherever you look. If you lose sight of your man, point at the lifebelt (what you do with the boat and how you recover the man, is dealt with in Chapter 8). If it is windy, the belt will blow across the

Lifebelt is attached to a light and drogue.

surface of the sea very quickly and the drogue helps to stop that happening. The belt marks the position of the casualty and gives him something to hang on to. The light is operated by a mercury switch once it is floating in the water. The lights have batteries, which should be checked regularly as part of your maintenance routine. Always check them before night cruising. If you carry two lifebelts with lights and throw them in one slightly after the other, you can use them as a transit to return to your man in the dark.

Heaving Line

A heaving line is a length of polypropylene with a knot at the end. It is used to throw to people in the water. Because it is made of polypropylene, it will float. Therefore, be careful that you do not end up with it around your propellers.

Life-Raft

Protection against the elements and stability is largely related to the size of the craft. Therefore, only get into a life-raft if you are absolutely sure your vessel is going to sink, or it is on fire and out of control. A life-raft is a small inflatable boat with a canopy, for use if you have to abandon your vessel. Take the life-raft out on deck, if it is not deck stowed, tie the painter on to the parent vessel (that is why you need to learn those knots), and when you are absolutely convinced that you need the life-raft, throw the whole thing over the leeward side of the vessel into the sea. It will weigh about 30 kilogrammes, but even so, it will float. Pull on the painter and approximately 10 metres of line will come out before it stops. At this point give a good hard tug

and that should activate the gas bottle and inflate the life-raft.

You still have hold of it by the painter, so bring it up to the boat and your crew can get into it. The bathing platform is probably the best place to board. Put the heaviest crew member in first. Try to get into the raft dry, as you will be more comfortable. You should all be in foul-weather gear and life-jackets. Take any other equipment that you feel may be useful, for example a hand-held VHF radio, flares, dinghy, torch, bottle of fresh water, etc.

Once in the liferaft, make a decision about cutting the painter. If possible, leave it attached to the vessel since it is much more conspicuous than the life-raft on its own. However, if your vessel is sinking, then cut the line and stream the drogue. Close the canopy, issue seasick tablets, tie the pump on and post a lookout. Anywhere within 40 or 50 nautical miles of the UK or Northern Continental coast, you will be in range of the Coast Guard. Providing you have made contact, you should expect to be rescued within an hour at the most. That could drop to twenty minutes in the Solent. If you do the majority of your cruising in sheltered waters and are never more than 2 or 3 nautical miles offshore, you might decide to carry an inflated dinghy instead of the life-raft. You can always hire a raft for your annual summer holiday.

Distress Flares

Red and orange flares are both ways of indicating distress. Keep flares in a waterproof container, somewhere easily accessible in an emergency. The recommendation for an offshore pack is four red hand-held flares, four red parachute flares and two orange smoke signals. They do have a limited life of a few years and should be disposed of sensibly. Please **do not** set them off on firework night.

Hand held red flares burn with a bright red flame. Set them off outside the vessel, according to the instructions on their side. Always stand on the leeward side of the vessel, so that the smoke is blown away from you. Use this type of flare when you are in sight of someone who may be able to help you, either on the coast or on another vessel.

Red parachute flares contain a rocket which takes the flare to around 300 metres. There, it ejects a bright red flare on a parachute, which comes back down to earth slowly. Because it is so high, it can be seen by people over the horizon. These flares should also be set off outside on the leeward side of the vessel. Fire two flares, one minute apart. Take great care as, like fireworks, they can kill if they hit a human being. Hold the flare firmly. It will make a lot of noise, so try not to jump as it is set off. Direct the flare slightly downwind, it is designed to climb back into the wind. In low cloud it is advisable to fire the flare downwind at 45 degrees so that the flare deploys under the cloud base.

Orange smoke signals are for daylight use and may be either hand held or floating. They are useful for aiding identification from the air and most say they are safe to use on petrol- or oil-covered water.

Marine VHF Radio

It is a legal requirement for anyone in charge of a marine VHF radio to hold an operator's certificate of competence. Safety of all at sea depends on correct use of the radio in general and the distress frequency in particular. Remember that the radio itself also needs to be licensed, thus giving the vessel a unique call sign for identification.

The term 'Distress' in the maritime world is given a very precise definition: there is grave and imminent danger to either a vessel or life. Under these circumstances you may make a distress signal. There are fifteen different ways of indicating distress at sea and they are all taken very seriously. You should therefore not use any of them just because you are having a bad day! The best way of signalling distress is a MAYDAY call on VHF channel 16. Keep the Mayday format to hand, along with a guide to operating your radio.

MAYDAY MAYDAY MAYDAY
THIS IS THE MOTOR VESSEL
IDENTIFICATION (THREE TIMES)
MAYDAY
IDENTIFICATION
POSITION
NATURE OF THE DISTRESS
ASSISTANCE REQUIRED
NUMBER OF PEOPLE ONBOARD
ANY OTHER INFORMATION
HELPFUL TO YOUR RESCUERS
OVER

The position of the vessel is of utmost importance and therefore comes at the start of the message. If you use a range and bearing it must be **from** the object of reference out to sea. This is the best option for coastal waters. If you use a latitude and longitude taken from an electronic navigation aid then state from which source. If you hear a Mayday while you are at sea, always write it down. If it is not responded to, transmit a Mayday Relay and pass the message on, or respond to the vessel and go to its assistance.

Digital Selective Calling (DSC) is the latest way of sending a distress call. This is all part of the new Global Maritime Distress and Safety System (GMDSS). If using VHF DSC, then channel 70 would be used. You should therefore not transmit voice on channel 70. GMDSS becomes mandatory for commercial craft in February 1999 and Holland, for example, will cease monitoring channel 16 for distress purposes. Again, an operator's licence is required for DSC.

First Aid Afloat

First aid is the same, whether ashore or afloat. However, the materials you have available on your boat are usually limited. You should endeavour to maintain an adequate first aid kit, which should include triangular bandages, prepared sterile dressings, assorted plasters, disposable gloves and we would add a small torch, resuscitation mask and a seasickness remedy. It is also advisable to carry aspirin in case someone onboard has a heart attack. Many of you will be at sea with only one or two crew, which can present a problem. The skipper is often the radio operator and possibly also the first aider. In addition, the elements can be unkind and the platform unstable. There are also obvious hazards associated with waterborne activities, especially in cold British Waters. Fortunately the VHF radio takes the place of the telephone and should be used with correct procedure and signals, as already mentioned.

Helicopter Rescue

At sea the helicopter can take the place of the ambulance, which again requires special procedures. Always make one member of your crew exclusively responsible for the VHF radio. There is nothing more frustrating for the helicopter crew than to keep calling a vessel whose radio is unmanned. Someone from the helicopter will brief you while they are still a long way off, as it is almost impossible to communicate once they are overhead. He

It is almost impossible to communicate when the helicopter is overhead.

The winchman will usually board on the port quarter.

19

will advise you to switch off your electronic navaid and tell you which course to steer and speed to maintain. You should write the instructions down and do as he asks if it is within your power. Clear the deck of anything which is likely to be affected by the downdraught. Remove your ensign staff if it is likely to get in the way of the winchman. He may drop a hi-line first, which you should not touch until it has earthed and discharged its static through the water or your deck. Never tie this line to your vessel. More commonly on a motor boat, he may just drop the winchman straight on to your port quarter.

Safety of the Vessel

Watertight Integrity

It is worth spending time identifying the hull openings in your vessel. Again, the time to do this is not when the vessel is filling up with water. Identify all of the sea cocks and exercise the mechanism at least once a month. It will be of little use knowing where to close a cock if it is corroded and seized, or the handle is missing. Sea cocks can seize up if they are left open all the time, which is not a pleasant fact to discover when you are taking in water. Other areas to check are the propeller shafts where they enter the vessel at the stern glands. The stern glands do need to weep slightly to avoid overheating. The rudder stock shafts and the log unit should also be checked. Some boats may have compartmentalization through the boat, with small bulkheads in the bilge and a pump in each section. Keep hatches and port lights closed when under way and also saloon windows in rough conditions.

Bilge Pumps

If you do spring a leak, the bilge pump is there to expel the water. These pumps are not designed to keep you afloat with a huge hole in the hull, only to deal with small leaks. Automatic electric pumps are best. Do not switch the breaker off when you leave your boat, because if you do they will no longer be automatic. Engine-driven bilge pumps are very efficient. Don't forget an effective bilge pump is a frightened person and a bucket!

Plugs

Soft wooden bungs should be carried onboard, to push into holes in the hull, for instance into the hole left when removing a log unit to clean the impeller. If the hole is larger and you do not have a large enough plug, put a cushion in a plastic bag over the hole and stand on it.

If you cannot keep the water under control, and there is a real danger of flooding the engine room, the last line of defence might be to run the boat on to a beach, if one is available. The cost could be new stern gear, but at least your crew can walk ashore in safety. Once a vessel has been to the bottom of the sea, there is a lot of work involved in repairing it.

The Head

The toilet onboard is known as the head. In the good old days, sailors would be subjected to the indignation of sitting over a hole at the head or bows of the ship when they felt the call of nature. The term has stuck, but fortunately not the custom! In modern heads sea water is sucked in through one sea cock, flushed around the bowl and pumped out through another sea cock, or into a holding tank. You should not put anything down a sea toilet which you have not eaten first, along with a small amount of toilet paper.

For using the toilet as a pump during emergencies, see the section on Sinking in Chapter 11.

Fire Prevention and Fire Fighting

Fire on a boat is even more serious than at home because you cannot just walk out into the garden to safety. Gas is a major cause of fire and should be handled with respect. It is important to manage the gas supply onboard to prevent leaks and possible explosions. Calor gas is heavy and will collect in the bilge, which is why we operate the bilge pump regularly and record it in the ship's log book. It is an added safety feature to have flame failure devices fitted to the cooker; these shut off the supply if the flame fails or if the taps are knocked open in rough weather. Strike your match before you turn on the tap and do not leave the cooker unattended when under way. It is very easy for something to fall on to the cooker with the movement of the boat. There will be a shut-off valve on the bottle itself and a main cock somewhere near the cooker. If you are using the cooker intermittently, it is acceptable to turn off the supply at the main cock and burn off the gas to the cooker. At the end of the day, turn off the gas at the bottle and burn off the gas in the system, before turning off the tap on the cooker.

Engine checks are an important way to find anything amiss in the engine room, which could be a cause of fire. For example, you may find a fuel leak or blocked sea-water strainers, which could cause

the exhaust pipes to overheat. It is advisable not to allow smoking below decks.

Dry powder extinguishers are ideal on a boat, as they can be used on any type of fire. The extinguisher is activated by pulling the lever as directed, thereby releasing the powder which smothers the fire. Make sure you carry enough of them and locate them near exits. The dry powder makes up about half of the content, the rest is a gas propellent. You should shake them every now and then, as the powder has a tendency to compact at the bottom of the extinguisher. They do make a horrible mess, but are very effective, non toxic and safe to use.

Halon or BCF extinguishers contain liquid under pressure. On activation, the extinguisher produces a greenish-yellow gas, which is very good at putting out fire but is harmful to you and the environment. These types of extinguisher, often automatic in engine room compartments, are gradually being withdrawn.

A **fire blanket** should be fitted to the bulkhead in the galley. It is used to smother pan fires and works by depriving the fire of oxygen. If a person's clothing is on fire, lie them on the ground to stop the flames rising to the face and head. Keep the burning side uppermost and cover the casualty in the blanket to smother the flames.

Engine Checks

There are those who seldom look under the bonnet of their car, and equally there are those who never look in the engine-room of their boat. We would suggest that this is a trifle foolhardy, since the engines are your only means of propulsion on a motor boat.

Sixty-two per cent of all launches by RNLI lifeboats to power craft are as a result of machinery failure. There were 1,508 launches to power pleasure craft in 1995. Included in this figure were 22 with an unsure position, 13 had steering failure, 31 caught fire, 53 ran out of fuel, but 861 were due to machinery failure.

There are checks to make on a daily basis, others while running and yet more less regularly.

Daily Checks

Every day before you set off, check that you have sufficient fuel for your intended passage. Always assume 20 per cent less than you have as a safety margin. Engine oil levels should be dipped and fresh-water coolant level and belt tension checked. Inspect your sea-water strainers and clean them if necessary. Also, look around your engine-room while you are down there, for oil, water and fuel leaks and stray nuts and bolts. It is a great advantage to have clean bilges, as it

becomes instantly obvious if you develop a small leak, or a nut or bolt vibrates free.

When all is ready, check that no ropes are hanging overboard near the propellers, ventilate the bilges and start the engines. Ensure that you have water exiting your exhausts, then you are ready to leave. This last step is not possible on outdrive engines. Do not leave diesel engines idling for too long; put them under load as soon as possible to warm them quickly and reduce wear and tear. Run petrol engines at fast idle until a reading appears on the temperature gauge to reduce the risk of stalling.

Running Checks

Make it part of your log routine to keep a note of engine temperature and oil

Sea-water strainers should be cleaned daily.

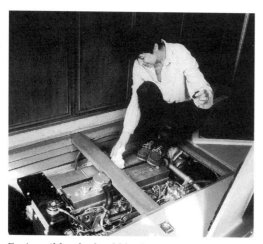

Engine oil levels should be dipped daily.

pressure. Also check that the batteries are charging and the fuel levels are as expected. If you are on a long passage, it does no harm to inspect the engines while underway. You should put on a pair of ear defenders before entering the engine compartment. Again, look for leaks and items vibrating free.

Do not run your engines at maximum rpm for long periods of time. For cruising reduce by at least 200/300rpm from maximum.

Weekly Checks

Drain any water from the fuel-filter water traps. If applicable, check trim tab, power tilt, gearbox and steering-gear oil levels. Grease the rudder stocks one turn and check the battery electrolyte levels. If you

The sea water impeller should be changed at intervals, according to manufacturer's instructions.

have a generator onboard, remember to check that engine as well. Check the stern glands for leaks, remembering that they do need a slow drip to function correctly.

Annual Checks

Refer to the engine manufacturer's handbook for annual maintenance items. These will probably include the following: the sea-water impeller should be changed, change gear box oil and filter if any, clean fuel lift pump strainer, renew fuel filters, clean or renew air filters and clean heat exchangers. Check the concentration of the coolant and remember that it acts as a corrosion inhibitor as much as an anti-freeze. When the boat is lifted, check sacrificial anodes.

Spares

Make sure you carry a supply of spare oil, oil filters, fuel pre-filters and fine filters, impeller, drive belt, and various clips, screws, pipes and sealing material. A tool kit is essential. Remember, you cannot call the AA and retire to the pub.

Summary

The conscientious skipper should be methodical and observant. Always give new crew members a thorough safety brief when they come onboard and ensure that there is adequate safety equipment for them. Much of your safety gear has an expiry date which should be regularly checked. The use of a maintenance log or check-list is a good idea. You should be familiar with your engine-room and keep it clean and tidy. This way, you are likely to notice when things go wrong and rectify them, thus preventing yourself from becoming a statistic.

Questions

1 When would you advise a crew member to wear a life-jacket?
2 When would you advise a crew member to wear a safety harness?
3 What is the order of information in a Mayday call and message?
4 What daily engine checks would you make?

Answers

1 When the crew members are non-swimmers, children or people who wish to do so. Other times would be when night cruising, during dinghy trips, when cruising in fog or rough weather or any other time when there is increased risk of falling overboard.
2 If you need to send someone on to the foredeck in rough conditions they should wear a safety harness as should a person recovering a man overboard. In very rough conditions a harness may be clipped around the flybridge seat.

3 MAYDAY MAYDAY MAYDAY

THIS IS THE MOTOR VESSEL

IDENTIFICATION (THREE TIMES)

MAYDAY

IDENTIFICATION

POSITION

NATURE OF THE DISTRESS

ASSISTANCE REQUIRED

NUMBER OF PEOPLE ONBOARD

ANY OTHER INFORMATION HELPFUL TO YOUR RESCUERS

OVER

4 Check that you have sufficient fuel for your intended passage. Engine oil levels should be dipped, coolant level, belt tension and sea-water strainers should be checked. Look around your engine-room for oil, water and fuel leaks and stray nuts and bolts. Start the engines and ensure that there is water exiting the exhausts from inboard engines.

3

SEAMANSHIP AND GENERAL
PRINCIPLES OF BOAT
HANDLING

Your crew should now be familiar with the safety equipment you carry and know how and when to use it. Next we will direct our attention to general seamanship and the basic principles of boat handling. When bringing a vessel into harbour, it is important to have warps and fenders ready. This entails the use of knots. It is also helpful to have a knowledge of the properties of rope so that the correct one can be chosen.

Knots

The RYA syllabus requires the Day Skipper to be able to tie a figure of eight, a reef knot, a bowline, a clove hitch, a rolling hitch, a round turn and two half hitches and a sheetbend. It is important to practise your knots so that you can execute them quickly when they are required. There is nothing worse for the novice skipper than to have the boat just ready for berthing, only to find the crew is still trying to remember how to tie on a fender! Even worse is the thought of somebody tying a life-raft on to the boat and throwing it overboard, only to see it drift away on the next wave. The following paragraphs will describe the various knots, though figure of eight or

stopper knots will not be covered as they are seldom required on motor boats.

Bowline

A bowline is used to make a non-slipping loop in a rope. It does not jam and is relatively easy to undo if it is not under load. It can always be undone, no matter how tight it has been pulled. Start with a loop in your left hand (if you are right-handed); it is important to have the rope overlapping at the front (see Fig 4). Then

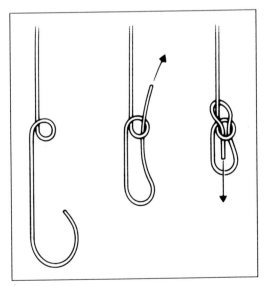

Fig 4   Bowline.

you must remember: 'the rabbit will come out of the hole, run round the back of the tree and disappear down the hole again.'

Clove Hitch

The clove hitch is easy to tie and quick to adjust, making it a suitable knot for securing fenders. Bring the rope over the guard rail and wrap it around once. Take the rope over itself and turn around the guard rail again, tucking the end through the loop which you have now created.

Pull tight. This knot is not very secure, so it is advisable to add a half hitch for security (see Fig 5).

Rolling Hitch

This is a knot that is difficult to remember and one that you will probably never use in anger. However, if you get into a situation where you need to take the strain off another rope, there is nothing else that will do the job as well. Wrap the end of the rope around the jammed rope,

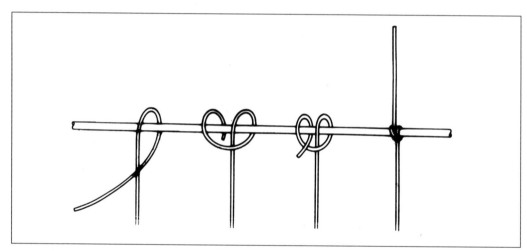

Fig 5 Clove hitch.

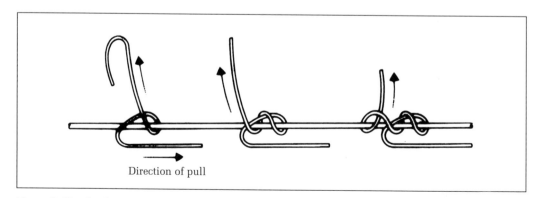

Direction of pull

Fig 6 Rolling hitch.

so that it crosses over itself, twice. Complete a third turn without crossing any other part of the knot and finish by passing the end under itself, as in Fig 6. The pull must be parallel to the jammed rope which will roll the knot.

Round Turn and Two Half Hitches

This is a very secure knot which may be used for attaching mooring lines. It is possible to let it go when it is under tension. Pass the rope over and through the object to which you want to secure. Pass it round again without crossing over itself. Make the two half hitches in the standing part of the rope as in Fig 7.

Sheetbend

Use a sheetbend, either single or double, to join two ropes of equal or unequal thickness. It is the same knot as a

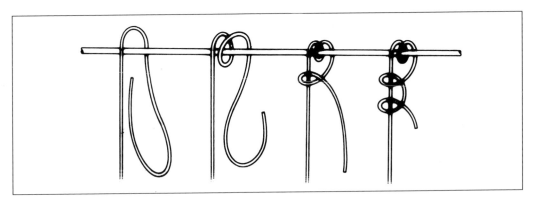

Fig 7   Round turn and two half hitches.

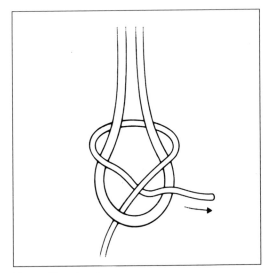

Fig 8   Sheet bend.

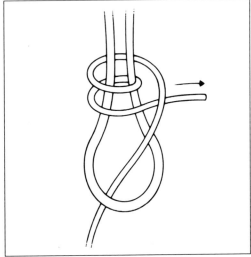

Fig 9   Double sheet bend.

27

Fig 10   Reef knot.

Coil ropes neatly after use.

bring it back, passing under itself, but not through the U again.

Reef Knot

Reef knots are used more for first aid than seamanship onboard a motor boat. You should learn how to tie one in case you have to apply a sling at any time! It is the simple left over right and under, right over left and under procedure as in Fig 10.

Ropework

There are four main types of modern synthetic rope. Nylon has the ability to stretch, absorb shock and it sinks in water. This makes it a good choice for mooring and anchor warps. Polypropylene is the cheapest rope and will float, making it ideal for rescue lines and painters. Polyester (Terylene) has very little stretch which makes it ideal for halyards on sailing vessels. Kevlar stretches even less, but is very expensive. Ropes may be constructed as a three-strand laid or twisted rope, which is the easiest to splice, or plaited or braided.

bowline, but without the loop. This means it has the same useful property in that it can always be undone, no matter how tight it has become. It may also be used to secure to an eye. Make a U in the end of the thicker rope. Bring the end of the thinner rope up through the U. Pass it round the back of the thicker rope and

Coils

It is a sign of good seamanship when you open a locker on a boat and see nicely coiled ropes. Your heart sinks when you see a locker full of macramé. If you coil ropes neatly every time you stow them, they are always ready for immediate use. This could be critical if you should need one in an emergency. To coil a rope, if you are right-handed, lay the rope across your left hand, make a loop of appropriate size and bring the rope across your hand again. You may need to roll the rope between the fingers of your right hand, if it has a tendency to twist in the loop. When you come to the end of your rope,

there are several ways to finish off. One option is to wrap the rope around the loops, near to your left hand, bring a loop through the small space left at the top and pass the end through it as in Fig 11.

Cleats

Always be aware of safety when working with cleats and keep your fingers as far away as possible. If warps are being used to manoeuvre a vessel, there could be a lot of strain on the rope so take plenty of turns on the cleat. When securing mooring lines, take the warp from the pontoon round the front of the cleat, then use a figure of eight and finish with a lock.

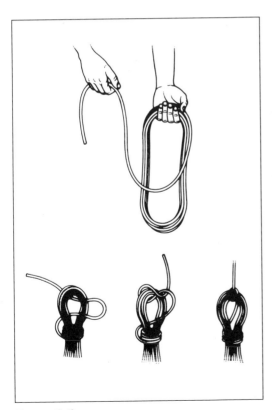

Fig 11   Coils.

The last thing you need when mooring is a tangle!

Take the spring from the pontoon, round the front of the cleat.

Apply figure of eights.

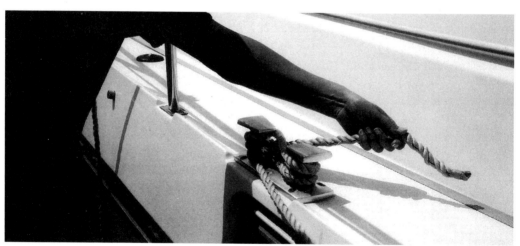

Finish with a locking turn.

The Bow Line

If you have a bow line ashore, you have perfect control over a twin-engined motor boat. Once the bow line is released, you are committed to your manoeuvre. So, when coming alongside, you need your bow line ashore first. Unless your crew is blessed with wings, do not ask them to leap off your bows into the great

unknown. They should attach a warp to the forward cleat, take it outside the guard rails and bring the end back onboard. They then stand ready on the bow with a coil of rope in each hand. When you bring the vessel up to the cleat on the pontoon, your crew can throw a loop ashore and tighten it with the end which is still onboard. Likewise, when you are leaving your berth, rig the bow line to slip and

A bow line gives you control over a twin-engined motorboat.

when you are ready to go, your crew can slip the rope, again from onboard.

Twin Shaft Drive Boat Handling

A single-engined displacement motor cruiser will have similar handling characteristics to a sailing yacht under auxiliary power. We will therefore concentrate on the twin-screw vessel, which is more common. Engines will be situated either side of the vessel's centre line, with small rudders behind the propellers which usually work in tandem, when the wheel is turned.

Turning Moment

If you go ahead on the port engine, because the push is not on the centre line, the boat will turn gently to starboard. This effect is called the turning moment (see Fig 12). If you have single-lever engine controls, looking at the configuration will

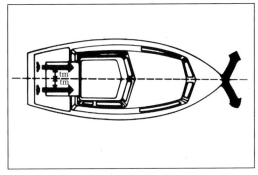

Fig 12 Turning moment.

help with this notion. If both engines are used together, this effect is cancelled out. The pivot point is the point around which the boat will naturally want to turn. The centre line is a line down the middle of the boat. Turning moment is the distance between the propeller shaft thrust line and the centre line.

Paddle Wheel Effect

Because the blades of a propeller are angled, they produce a screwing effect through the water when the propeller is

Single-lever engine controls.

turned. This gives the vessel its drive. Imagine a twin-bladed propeller, moving in a clockwise direction. As the propeller turns, the top blade moves left to right and meets the resistance of the water. This will produce a reactive force on the propeller shaft to the left. The lower blade moves right to left and produces a similar reactive force on the shaft to the right. The obvious thought is that the two will cancel each other out. However, since the top blade is nearer the surface of the water, it experiences less water resistance than the bottom blade which is in deeper water (see Fig 13). You could demonstrate this by moving water with your hand near

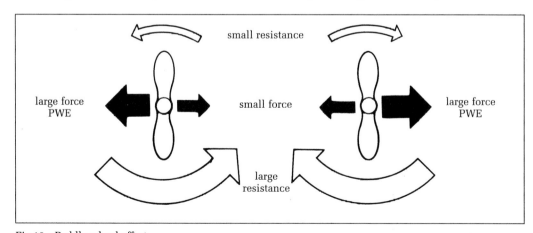

Fig 13   Paddle wheel effect.

the surface and then trying to walk through it, which would be harder to do. Thus, the lower blade, being in deeper water, generates a bigger sideways force. The result of this, is that the propeller tries to 'paddle wheel' sideways, as well as screwing forwards through the water. The lower blade may also be experiencing less turbulence, as this is more prevalent near the surface, which may further increase the sideways effect.

Twin-engined vessels will usually have the propellers arranged to be outward turning when viewed from astern; i.e. starboard turns clockwise and port turns anti-clockwise. When both engines are put ahead the paddle wheel effects are cancelled. So, if you put only your port engine ahead, you will now have the turning moment effect being supplemented by the paddle wheel effect to increase the turn to starboard. If the propeller turned inwards, paddle wheel effect would cancel the turning moment. Faireys have a different propeller configuration. They usually have both propellers turning the same way. It is important to know which way the propellers turn on the vessel which you are handling.

Slip-Stream Effect

When a propeller is turning in forward motion, water is taken from in front of it and forced out of the back. If there is a rudder positioned at an angle behind the propeller, the stream of water will be deflected by the rudder, generating a force on the rudder. This will also assist the boat to turn and is called the slip-stream effect. This effect is reduced at slow speed and in proportion to the size of the rudder. Note that the rudders have very

little effect when the engines are running astern.

Turning the Boat in a Confined Space

It is possible to turn a twin-screw motor cruiser in its own length. Put one engine ahead and one astern at the same time. For example, the port engine pushing ahead tries to turn the bows to starboard. The starboard engine pulling astern tries to bring the stern round to port. Paddle wheel effect and turning moment will all be working to help the turn. If you put the helm over as well, in favour of the engine which is going ahead, then you will get some slip stream effect from the rudder to help the turn (see Fig 14). If possible, the novice is advised to work just with the engine controls at first and keep the wheel for windy days.

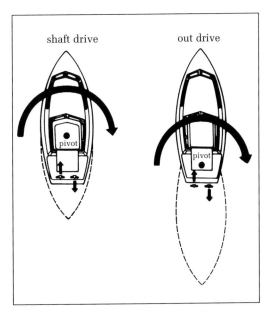

Fig 14 A shaft drive boat almost turns in own length. An outdrive boat requires two boat lengths to turn.

If both engines are working at the same speed, as the vessel comes round she will probably tend to creep forward. This happens because the propeller design is optimized for working ahead and the sharp bows are easier to move than the slab-shaped stern. Simply take the ahead engine out of gear for a moment and the astern engine will pull you back. Likewise, if you find yourself moving backwards too far, take the astern engine out of gear. Initially this is preferable to applying more power, as it produces a more sedate and controlled turn. Once you start giving more power to correct manoeuvres, movement speeds up and there is a tendency to start using handfuls of power as the situation gets out of control. The only thing this is sure to produce is a bigger repair bill!

Windage

Until now, we have not given the wind any consideration. When you first take a boat out, find a stretch of open water and try to establish how it will react to the wind. Left to their own devices, most high-sided motor craft will tend to lie more or less beam on (sideways) to the wind and be displaced sideways at something like 10 per cent of the wind speed. This is useful information to bear in mind when boat handling in confined areas.

It is very difficult to hold the bows into a wind of any strength. If you need to hover in a strong wind, then turn the boat stern into the wind, as it is much more controllable. When you have bows to the wind, as soon as the wind gets to one side, the vessel will swing round quickly. It takes longer for the wind to get hold of the stern.

Once you are beam on to the wind, you have no control over the sideways motion. The engines can move the vessel forward or backward and produce a turn, but they cannot move the vessel sideways. So let us imagine that you are caught beam on to the wind and you are being pushed sideways towards a pontoon. Turn the bows towards the danger and back away into the wind. Initially go astern on the inside engine. Paddle wheel effect pulls the stern away from the danger; it will tend to pull the bows in, but the bows are curved and overhang, so you will have a much better chance of not hitting the pontoon. Putting the outside engine ahead at the same time will pivot the boat more quickly if you are really in trouble. This is not an instinctive reaction. Folk tend to want to drive themselves forward out of danger as they would in a car. By driving forward out of a tight spot, the stern is being pushed sideways towards the obstruction with all the power of the engines. In addition, there will be the paddle wheel and turning moment effects acting against you. If contact is made serious damage could result.

Outdrive Boat Handling

Outdrive vessels do not have rudders. Instead, the whole leg moves in order to give direction to the propellers. This means that you definitely do need to use the wheel to get maximum manoeuvrability. There will still be a turning moment effect, due to the fact that there is one leg sited either side of the vessel's centre line. If single propellers are fitted, there will be paddle wheel effect. However, if the legs are fitted with duo props, where two

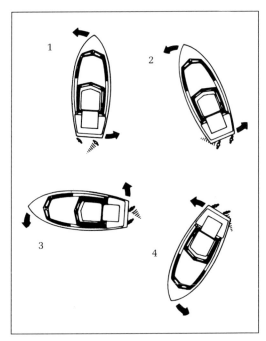

Fig 15 Alternative method for outdrive boat. 1 Starboard engine ahead, port helm. 2 Port engine astern starboard helm. Keep stern swing going. 3 Starboard engine ahead port helm. 4 etc!

method is highly recommended when learning. It gives a very controlled and gentle turn and has the further advantage of minimizing confusion in the mind of the helmsman! Concentration is applied solely to the engine controls and the helm is left alone.

The main drawback to the 'engines only' method of turning is that, as we have already mentioned, with outdrives, paddle wheel effects are generally small and the position of the propellers, aft of the transom, makes this a rather inefficient system. With a good wind blowing, the turning effects may not be strong enough to bring her round. An alternative method for outdrive vessels is to shuffle, or 'back and fill' as it is correctly termed. For a turn to port, start with full port helm, then engage the starboard engine ahead. The initial effect will be to start the stern swinging to starboard. Next, before the boat gathers any appreciable forward motion, go into neutral, apply full starboard helm and engage the port engine astern. This will continue the stern swing to starboard and remove forward motion. Before the boat gathers any appreciable stern motion, go into neutral, apply full port helm and engage the starboard engine ahead. To keep the swing going, change to port engine astern with starboard wheel and so on until the turn is complete. Use full lock each time and turn the wheel to the new position **before** engaging the engine (see Fig 15).

propellers are fitted to the same leg, each turning in opposite directions, there will be only a very small paddle wheel effect.

To turn an outdrive boat in a confined space, it is perfectly feasible to adopt the method used for the shaft drive boat above. With helm amidships, put one engine ahead and one astern. The boat will turn slowly around. As above, adjustments will need to be made to prevent the boat creeping forward. This

Summary

Practise your knots and have a selection of warps coiled and stowed ready for use. Teach your crew how to throw a bow line ashore from onboard and how to attach fenders correctly. When using one engine, turning moment will usually combine with paddle wheel effect, because the propellers are offset and this will generate a turn. With high topsides, wind may be a predominant consideration outweighing the tidal effect. Motor boats generally want to lie beam on to the wind, but are more controllable if they are stern to wind. Always use the least amount of power necessary to execute your manoeuvre in the prevailing conditions, do not use frantic bursts of throttle, or try to drive yourself out of trouble.

Questions

1 There are four main types of modern synthetic rope. What are they and which would you choose for mooring lines?

2 Is it advantageous to have your propellers turning outward or inward when going ahead?

3 Why could it be wrong to try to drive a boat forwards out of danger?

Answers

1 Nylon, Polypropylene, Polyester (Terylene) and Kevlar. Nylon has the ability to stretch and absorb shock. This makes it a good choice for mooring warps.

2 Outward turning, as the turning moment will combine with paddle wheel effect to assist with boat handling. If propellers were inward turning the two effects would cancel each other out.

3 Let us once again imagine that you are caught beam on to the wind and that you are being pushed sideways towards a pontoon. If you tried to drive the vessel forwards out of danger, you would need to put your inside engine ahead. Paddle wheel effect, turning moment and slip-stream effect would all combine to ram the stern of your vessel into the pontoon.

4

THEORETICAL REVISION

In this chapter we will revise the information contained on a chart and the various types of chart available. We will go on to revise basic navigation; that is, determining where you are, where you want to go and how you will get there. To do this you will use plotting instruments, position lines and tidal vectors.

Navigation Charts

A chart is a representation of the sea bed with depths drawn to the level of chart datum, which is the lowest astronomical tide. The coastline is represented together with significant features ashore which may be visible from seaward.

Makes of Chart

There are various makes of chart available on the market. Charts are produced by the Hydrographic Department of the Admiralty for use primarily by the Royal Navy, but are also sold commercially. Stanford Maritime and Imray, Laurie, Norie and Wilson base their charts on Admiralty surveys, but edit the information specifically for pleasure craft use. Electronic charts are becoming more readily available these days as technology

advances and sailors want to take their computers to sea. However, the RYA courses are still based on paper charts and Admiralty charts are considered by many to be the best.

Scale

The scale is the relationship between a given distance on the chart and the actual distance it represents on the earth's surface. There are many different scales produced. They are usually represented by a ratio, where for example 1:100,000 means that one centimetre on the chart corresponds to 100,000 centimetres on the earth's surface. If a mile is small on the chart, it is a small-scale chart and is used to plan passages whereas large-scale charts are useful when detail is required, for example harbour plans.

Projection

There are two types of projection used in chart construction. Most navigational charts are mercator projection, where a compass course always appears as a straight line and the meridians of latitude and parallels of longitude form a rectangular grid.

Mercator projection converts the

Earth's surface from a globe to a cylinder. Imagine a light bulb has been placed in the centre of the Earth casting an image on to a tube of paper wrapped round it. The chart is then traced from the image. There will be a lot of distortion at the North and South Poles. The parallels of latitude will increase in separation from the equator to the pole. As one minute on the latitude scale is equal to one nautical mile, it is important to use the scale opposite your working position to obtain accurate distance.

Gnomonic projection views the Earth as a flattened surface at a tangent to the Earth, as viewed from a point at the centre of the Earth. Meridians of longitude converge towards the poles and parallels of latitude appear as curves. This projection is very accurate for large-scale charts.

Information Available on an Admiralty Chart

Each chart has a specific catalogue number to identify it and a title describing the area of coverage. Under the title there will be information about the soundings either in metres, which are more common, or fathoms which are still used in a few areas that have not been updated. The scale will be noted, as described above. There will be information on depths, which are usually referenced to chart datum, and on heights, which are either drying heights if underlined, or measured above Mean High Water Springs. The type of projection will be mentioned and there may also be a list of cautions. Along the bottom will be a list of corrections and new editions. Chart corrections are published four times a year as the *Small Craft Edition of the Notices to Mariners*. You should keep your charts corrected up to date. The scales of latitude and longitude will surround the chart and there will be a compass rose with details of variation which changes from year to year. The symbols and abbreviations on these charts will be found in the Admiralty publication 5011.

Metric Charts

Land is shown in yellow and drying areas in green. Inshore waters less than five, ten or twenty metres according to the scale of

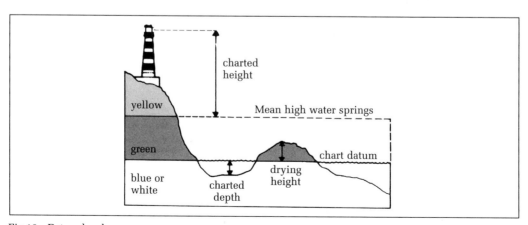

Fig 16   Datum levels.

the chart are marked in blue. Deeper water is shown in white. Fig 16 shows the datum levels more clearly.

Symbols Used When Plotting on Charts

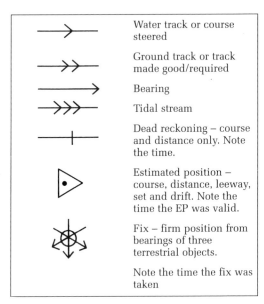

→	Water track or course steered
→»	Ground track or track made good/required
→	Bearing
→»»	Tidal stream
—+—	Dead reckoning – course and distance only. Note the time.
▷	Estimated position – course, distance, leeway, set and drift. Note the time the EP was valid.
⊕	Fix – firm position from bearings of three terrestrial objects. Note the time the fix was taken

Fig 17.

Plotting Instruments

There are various patterns of plotting instruments available. The Breton-type plotter or Portland plotter tend to be favoured by many motor boaters. Variation can be marked on the scale of these plotters so that it is applied in the correct direction. Another benefit is that you can work on a small area of chart, without the need to refer to the compass rose for a bearing. Protractors are preferred by other skippers. Parallel rules can be difficult to use with the motion of a motor boat, though some skippers will swear by them. Work with something with which you are comfortable, because comfort and accuracy are the most important factors. In addition, you will also need a pair of dividers. Single-handed dividers are preferred by many.

Compasses, Variation and Deviation

The Magnetic Compass

A magnetic compass has a magnetic needle which lines up with the Earth's magnetic field. It will always point in the same direction, to the magnetic pole, regardless of the ship's heading. This characteristic enables you to measure the course steered by your vessel. Have your compass swung by a qualified compass adjuster and check it against a known transit occasionally.

Causes of Compass Errors

1   Poor siting of compass – too close to engines, electronic equipment, etc.
2   Poor initial compass swing or change in deviation.

A Breton-type plotter in use.

3 Lubbers line not aligned with ship's centre line.

4 Small iron objects placed too near the compass, perhaps temporarily.

5 Local magnetic anomalies, usually indicated on the chart.

6 Using a hand-bearing compass while wearing metal-framed spectacles for example.

Variation

The error between Magnetic North and True North (the geographic Pole) is called **variation**. Variation changes with position on the Earth's surface and can be either East or West. It is always marked on the compass rose of a chart but be careful to check the date, as it changes by a few minutes each year.

Deviation

Metal objects on the boat, specifically iron objects, will influence the compass, causing deviation. Deviation alters according to the ship's heading.

Types of Bearing

A True bearing relates to the geographic pole.

A Magnetic bearing relates to the magnetic pole with variation but no deviation applied.

A Compass bearing relates to the magnetic pole with variation and any deviation applied.

All bearings which are given on charts, e.g. light sectors, leading lines, tidal streams etc. are TRUE bearings.

Adjusting a Compass for Deviation

A compass adjuster will **swing** the compass to measure deviation and using corrector magnets in the compass will reduce deviation to a minimum. He then produces a **deviation card** of residual error. GRP boats with a well-located compass can expect a maximum deviation of one or two degrees. A 'bad' example can be twenty to thirty degrees on an 'unswung' compass. On iron or

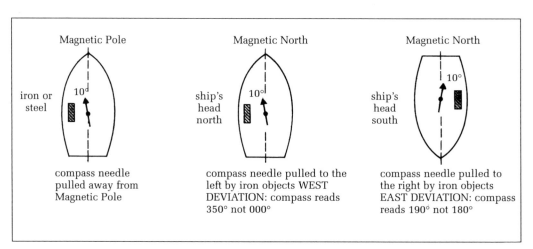

Fig 18.

steel ships, the compass compensation is a complicated exercise and will usually be the subject of an annual compass swing by a qualified compass adjuster.

DEVIATION CHANGES WITH HEADING AND CAN BE EAST OR WEST.

There is a rule to help remember how to apply variation and deviation.

CADET RULE

Compass to True ADd East

C ☞ T   ADE

	Deviation		Variation	
Compass	———	Magnetic	———	True
	Add East		Add East	
	Subtract West		Subtract West	

Cadbury's Dairy Milk Very Tasty

	Variation		Deviation	
True	———	Magnetic	———	Compass
	Subtract East		Subtract East	
	Add West		Add West	

True Virgins Make Dull Companions

Fig 19.

Causes of Change in Deviation

1 Change in position of iron/steel objects onboard, for example outboard motors.

2 Changes in the vessel's magnetic field caused by:

i. major repairs to hull and or superstructure

ii. changes to onboard equipment location

iii. heavy shocks to the vessel as in rough weather or grounding

iv. lightning strikes or heavy-current short circuits

Constructing Tidal Vectors

Always work on the chart in True and convert to Compass before giving the bearings to your helmsman.

Dead Reckoning and Estimated Position

It is 1030 hrs and you are in a position marked A, which you have established from a three-bearing fix. From this position you steer a course of 090°T for one hour, in which time you cover a distance of twenty miles. A course steered or water track is marked by one arrow. With no allowance for leeway, set or drift, your position at 1130 hrs would be at B. This is called **dead reckoning**.

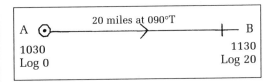

Fig 20   Dead reckoning.

Now let us imagine that a North wind is blowing for the duration of this trip and it pushes the boat off course by 5°. This effect is known as **leeway**. The track of the boat through the water becomes 095°T if you take leeway into account (see Fig 21).

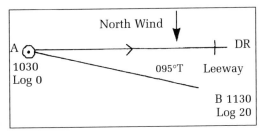

Fig 21   Leeway.

We will also imagine that there is a tidal stream flowing in the direction of 195°T at a rate of five knots. Plot this from the end of the water track, for the amount of time that you have travelled. In this case it is one hour, so you allow five miles of tide for this passage and mark it as tidal input by adding three arrows (see Fig 22).

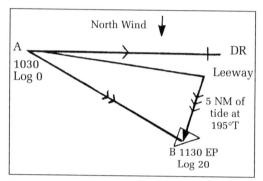

Fig 22.

Dead reckoning is not very accurate as you can see. By taking account of the wind and tide that have affected the boat during the past hour, you end up in a very different position. The resultant line is your **track made good**, shown by adding two arrows, and B is your **estimated position**.

Course to Steer

When working out your course to steer, a triangle is drawn for the most convenient period of time. First you must work out the approximate duration of your passage from A to B at a speed which you think you can safely achieve. Draw this **track to be made good** on the chart.

For this example, you have a track to be made good of twenty-two miles, at an assumed speed of twenty knots. This will take a little over one hour to achieve (see Fig 23).

Next, work out the tidal direction and rate

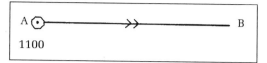

Fig 23.

for the hour from 1100–1200, either by using an almanac, a tidal stream atlas or the nearest tidal diamond on the chart. Remember to use the tidal data for half an hour either side of the time stated. Apply this tide at position A, assuming 180°T at five knots for this exercise. Draw AC, direction 180°T, length 5 nautical miles.

Now open your dividers to the distance that the boat will travel through the water in one hour, using the latitude scale opposite your position. Put one point of your dividers on the end of your tidal line and make a pencil mark where the other point cuts the **track to be made good**. Joining the end of your tidal line to the mark you have just made, will give you the course to steer. If you need to allow for leeway, do this now, by altering the angle into the wind, say 3° (see Fig 24).

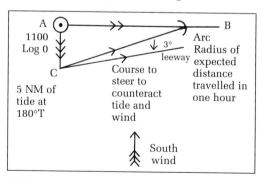

Fig 24.

When working out courses to steer, always work in convenient periods of time and never join the end of your tidal set and drift to your final destination. Before giving your course to steer to the

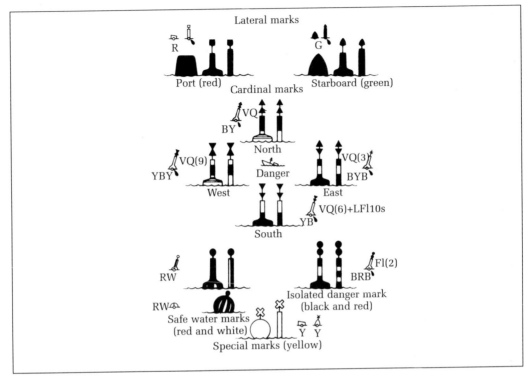

Fig 25.

helmsman, add Variation and Deviation and round the figure up or down (away from any hazards) to the nearest 5°. It is easier to steer 150° than 148.75°!

The following may be helpful when calculating speed, time or distance:

$$\text{SPEED} = \frac{\text{DISTANCE}}{\text{TIME}} \qquad \text{TIME} = \frac{\text{DISTANCE}}{\text{SPEED}}$$

$$\text{DISTANCE} = \text{SPEED} \times \text{TIME}$$

Buoyage

IALA system A is the system of buoyage which is used around the UK and Western Europe. System B is used in America. Buoys impart a lot of information to the skipper by night and day.

Light Characteristics

Any object which has a light will be marked on the chart with a magenta flash. There are a number of characteristics which these lights may exhibit:

Fixed lights (F) are on all the time.
Flashing lights (Fl) are off longer than on. They may be group flashing, for example, Fl (3) 10s, where the light would flash three times every ten seconds.
Long flashing (L Fl) where the flash is two seconds or longer.
Quick flashing (Q) usually flash either fifty or sixty times per minute.
Very quick flashing (VQ) usually flash either 100 or 120 times per minute.
Occulting lights (Oc) are on longer than

they are off.

Isophase lights (Iso) have an equal duration of light and dark.

Where the height and range of a light are of importance, as for a lighthouse, the height is in metres (m) and the range in miles (M). Lights may also be sectored, in which case they may not be visible through 360 degrees.

There are five groups of buoys, which are shown in Fig 25: cardinal marks, lateral marks, isolated danger, safe water and special marks. It should be noted that buoys are not always lit and not necessarily in the exact position that they are shown on the chart.

Cardinal Marks

The four cardinal marks are designed to protect you from specific navigational hazards. They represent the four cardinal points of a compass – North, South, East and West – with the hazard assumed to be in the middle. You should therefore pass North of a North cardinal mark and so on. They are usually pillar buoys, but can be posts and all have yellow and black horizontal stripes. The cones point to the black stripes on the buoys for easy daytime identification if you are too far away to see the top marks. A North cardinal will therefore have a top mark consisting of two cones pointing upward and a corresponding black stripe at the top of the buoy. However, if the bottom of this buoy was dirty and covered in seaweed, it could be possible to mistake it for an East cardinal with black stripes at the top and bottom. It is always best to identify the top mark if possible. Their lights, if fitted, will be white. The flashing sequence loosely follows the numbering on a clock face: three flashes for East, six plus one

long flash for South, nine for West and continuous for North.

A South cardinal buoy.

Lateral Marks

Lateral marks are used to buoy the edge of a navigable channel. Red cans to port and green cones to starboard when you are entering the channel from seaward. Lights, if fitted, match the colour of the buoy and may be flashing in any rhythm.

Isolated Danger Marks

Isolated danger marks buoy a specific point of danger. They have safe water all around them. The buoy may be of pillar or spar shape and will have black and red horizontal stripes, with two black balls as the top mark. The light will be white, group flashing two.

Safe Water Marks

Safe water marks show navigable water with no specific hazards in the area. The buoy may be of spherical, pillar or spar shape and will have white and red vertical stripes. The top mark will be one red ball and the light white, either isophase, occulting or one long flash every ten seconds.

Special Marks

Special marks are not used for navigation, but to show spoil grounds, historical wrecks, recreation areas such as water ski areas, military exercise grounds and racing marks. They may be any shape, yellow and have a yellow X as a top mark. Lights will be yellow if carried, with any rhythm which does not conflict with nearby white navigational lights.

Summary

Your choice of chart will depend very much on the amount of cruising that you do and the space available on your vessel. If you have a full-size chart table and spend a lot of time afloat, your choice may be Admiralty charts. However, if space is limited, you might choose one of the fold-away varieties. Have your compass 'swung' and display your deviation card. Make a note of variation and mark it on your plotter if you have the facility to do so. When working out courses to steer, always work in convenient periods of time and never join the end of your tidal set and drift to your final destination. Before giving your course to steer to the helmsman, add Variation and Deviation to the True Water Track.

Questions

1 Why is it important to use the latitude scale opposite your position when measuring distance?

2 What do the following symbols represent when used on a navigation chart?
   a) ——→——   b) ——→→——
   c) ————→   d) ——→→→——
   e) ———+———   1100 log 12
   f) ▷ 1300 log 25

g) 🧭 0900 log 0

3 What is the CADET rule?
4 Why is dead reckoning not very accurate?
5 When working out courses to steer, would you join the end of your tidal set and drift to your final position to find your course?
6 What do the cardinal marks tell you?

Answers

1 Mercator projection converts the Earth's surface from a globe to a cylinder. The parallels of latitude will increase in separation from the equator to the pole. As one minute on the latitude scale is equal to one nautical mile, it is important to use the scale opposite your working position to obtain accurate distance.

2. a) ——→——   Water track or course steered
   b) ——→→——   Ground track or track made good/required
   c) ————→   Bearing
   d) ——→→→——   Tidal stream
   e) ———+———   Dead reckoning – course and distance only
   f) ▷ Estimated position – course, distance, leeway, set and drift
   g) 🧭 Fix – firm position from bearings of three terrestrial objects.

3 The cadet rule helps you remember whether to add or subtract variation. Compass to True ADd East.
   C 🖙 T ADE

4 Dead reckoning is not very accurate because it does not take into account the wind and tide that have affected the boat during the passage.

5 When working out courses to steer, always work in convenient periods of time and never join the end of your tidal set and drift to your final position. Put one point of your dividers, set to your expected boat speed for the relevant time, on the end of your tidal line. With the other point, make an arc to cut the track to be made good and make a pencil mark.

6 The four cardinal marks are designed to protect you from specific navigational hazards and mark the cardinal points of the compass.

5

PLANNING YOUR PASSAGE

In this chapter we will look at the planning which you should undertake before you make your passage. You may even choose to complete the bulk of this process at home. We will cover standard and secondary tidal calculations and sources of planning and pilotage information. Lastly, we will revise meteorology and the forecast information available to you.

Where Shall We Go?

When deciding on a destination you should always consider the crew that you will be taking with you, as well as the more nautical factors. It is often said that the crew will let you down long before the vessel. Do not be too ambitious, build up confidence slowly, or you could find that you have to take up single-handed cruising!

Gathering Information

Once you have decided on a destination, gather as much information as you can before you start your plan. Make sure that you have the appropriate scale **charts** for the area which you intend to visit and that they are corrected to date. You will need small-scale charts for planning and large-scale charts for the detail of harbours and entrances. Have ready any relevant publications giving information on local regulations, potential hazards and navigation lights, in **almanacs** or **pilot** books for example. Information about VHF and berthing procedures is also useful. Tidal information can be obtained from the almanac, or you may have specific **tide tables** and **tidal stream atlases**. Note down times and sources of **weather information** which you intend to monitor.

Information About Your Vessel

Make a note of the fuel capacity, maximum fuel consumption and range of the vessel. Remember to assume twenty per cent less than the fuel onboard for a safety margin when planning. Find out the draught of the vessel and also the air draught if you are intending to go under low bridges. If possible, find out from where the echo sounder measures, but if you cannot, then assume it is reading from the water line for safety.

Charts

Look at the charts and draw a line indicating the route which you intend to take. Note down any navigational hazards to avoid *en route*. Mark any changes of course to avoid these hazards. For the purpose of this exercise, we will imagine a weekend away on your boat in the Solent. You will start with a passage from the River Hamble to Cowes on the first day.

Hamble to Cowes General Information

Leave Hamble on a transit, leaving Hamble Point Buoy to starboard.

Change course to pass
  Hook QG (horn (1) 15s) – Green channel marker. (Port)
  Cross main shipping channel with care and run outside of the main channel.
  Black Jack Fl(2) R 4s – Red channel marker. (Port)

Change course at Black Jack.
  Head for Castle Point IQR 10s – Red channel marker. (Port)

Change course at Castle Point.
  Head for Calshot Spit Fl 5s 12m 11M (horn (2) 60s) – Red light float/white light. (Port)

Change course at Calshot Spit.
  Pass Bourne Gap Fl R 3s to Port.
  Run on until you see West Bramble Cardinal to port VQ(9) 10s (Racon, Bell).

Change course.
  Run into Cowes.

(In good visibility you could turn for Cowes at Bourne Gap, taking care to avoid Spanker yellow buoy which is unlit).

Skipper's Notes

Charts

2022 Harbours and Anchorages in the Eastern Solent

1905 Southampton Water and Approaches
2793 Cowes Harbour and River Medina

Other skippers prefer to have a more pictorial guide (fig 26), together with the following:

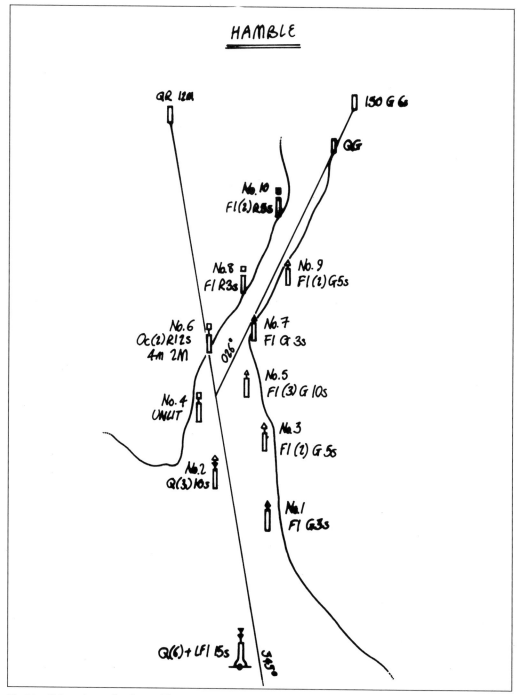

Fig 26 Skipper's notebook Hamble.

PORT	DISTANCE AND COURSE TO STEER	STARBOARD
		Hamble Point South Cardinal Q (6) + LFl 15s
Hook – Green channel marker QG (horn (1) 15s)	.7 M	
Cross main shipping channel with care and run outside of the main channel		
Black Jack – Red channel marker Fl(2) R 4s	.4 M Change course	
Castle Point – Red channel marker IQR 10s	.5 M Change course	
Calshot Spit – Red light float /white light Fl 5s 12m 11M (horn (2)60s)	.38 M Change course	
Bourne Gap – Red channel marker Fl R 3s		
West Bramble Cardinal VQ(9) 10s (Racon, Bell)	1.2 M Change course	
No. 4 – Red channel marker QR	1.5 M	No. 3 – Green channel marker Fl G 3s

Pilotage Information

If you are setting off from a harbour or marina which is unfamiliar, you will need to gather information for your departure point and destination.

Information found on the navigation chart

If you are making a long trip, you need to look at the chart for tidal races which you should negotiate at a specific time. You also need to identify bolt holes in case you have to abandon your trip. Lighthouses, racons and buoys can also be noted. As you are staying within the Solent for your fictitious passage, these are not a consideration on this occasion.

You should look at a large-scale chart of the area for any leading lines and note any buoys that you would see on your passage into the river or harbour. Work out the minimum water which you could expect on that day, in any shallow water areas or over bars.

Information found in books

Next, move on to any books which you have to assist you. Again, the almanac is useful along with any pilot books you might have. Start gathering information for Cowes. In the almanac there is advice on shelter, navigation, lights and marks, radio telephone and facilities, all of which is worth reading. Find information to help you enter safely if you have not been before, for example there are leading lights at night. Check all this information against the chart to give you a clearer

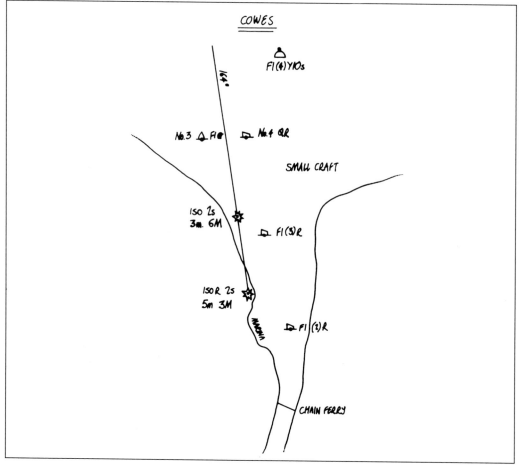

Fig 27   Skipper's notebook, Cowes.

picture. Start building up a pilot book of your own. Note any facts which you feel are important and draw yourself a sketch which you can take on deck with you. This information can also be gathered for other intended destinations over the weekend.

Electronic Information

If you use electronic navigation systems on your boat, work out some suitable waypoints. If your system is portable, you could program them in at home.

Skipper's Notes for Cowes

Shelter Good, but outer harbour exposed to N and NE winds.

Hazards Bramble bank dries 1.3m to the North. Mud flats and small craft moorings are to the East. Car ferries, hydrofoils and catamarans operate from just inside the entrance.

Navigation Leading lights 164° bring you safely in. Front light Iso 2s 3m 6M and back light Iso R 2s 5m 3M, visible 120° − 240°.
Green (No3 Fl G 3s) and red (No4 QR) buoys mark the entrance near W shore. Yachts must use the main channel and are advised to motor. The speed limit in the harbour is 6 knots.
VHF All yachts are advised to monitor Ch 69 Cowes Harbour Radio. Marinas use Ch 80. Water taxis listen on Ch 08.
Moorings Visitors' buoys, piles, public pontoon and several marinas.
Facilities There is fuel available and a variety of yacht clubs.

Tidal Information

Now look up the tidal height information and write it down in your skipper's notebook as follows. Your first port of call is Cowes, which you should look up in the almanac. You will notice that information for Cowes itself and the tidal

stream information for the Solent are based on Portsmouth data.
Find the information for your first day. There will be a note which says 'time zone UT, for summer time add one hour in non-shaded areas'; do not forget to do this if it applies. Of course you would only work calculations for the times which were relevant to you, but for practice we will correct for the whole day.

Portsmouth

	Time	m	BST
1	0347	0.8	0447
SA	1041	4.6	1141
	1606	0.8	1706
	2301	4.7	0001

Next, work out the ranges by subtracting the heights of low from high water. Using our example, these are 3.8m and 3.9m respectively. Look at the Portsmouth curve and you will find the mean spring range is 3.9m. So, you will be working with spring tides on this particular day. Spring tides, remember, have the greatest high and smallest low tidal heights.

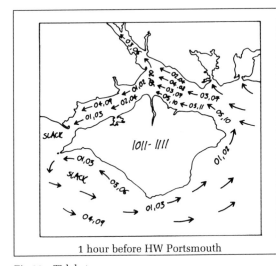

1 hour before HW Portsmouth

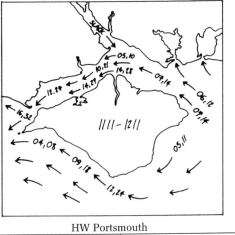

HW Portsmouth

Fig 28   Tidal streams.

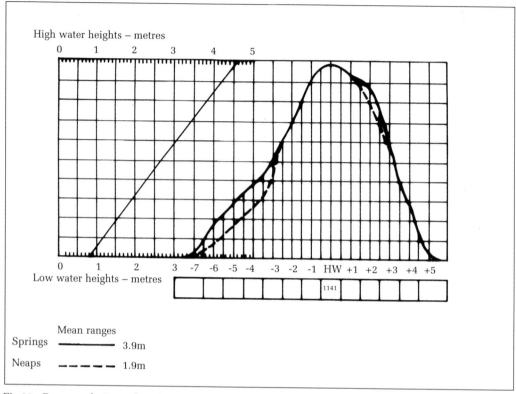

Fig 29 Portsmouth. Example only – not to be used for tidal calculations afloat.

Set up the tidal stream pages, by writing the time in each square in pencil as in Fig 28. High water is 1141 BST and you will use the 'high water Portsmouth' data for half an hour before and after this time, that is between 1111 hrs and 1211 hrs. You could also set up the Portsmouth tidal curve for the first day, by marking the low and high water heights and joining them with a pencil line as in Fig 29. Add the relevant high water time. Fig 30 should help you interpret the information shown on the tidal curve.

Now turn your attention to the heights and times of high and low water at Cowes. Information is found for Cowes and the River Medina. First, look at times in GMT.

Times			Height (metres)	
High	Low	MHWS		MLWN
Water	Water		MHWN		MLWS
0000 0600	0500 1100	4.7	3.8	1.9	0.8
1200 1800	1700 2300				

Differences Cowes

−0015 +0015	0000 −0020	−0.5	−0.3	−0.1	0.0

First Low Water at Portsmouth is 0347 GMT. That falls within the 2300 to 0500 band, which covers six hours, with differences moving from −20 minutes to 00 minutes. The correction is therefore reduced by 3.33 minutes per hour, (20 ÷ 6).

Your correction is 4 hours 47 minutes after 2300 hours.

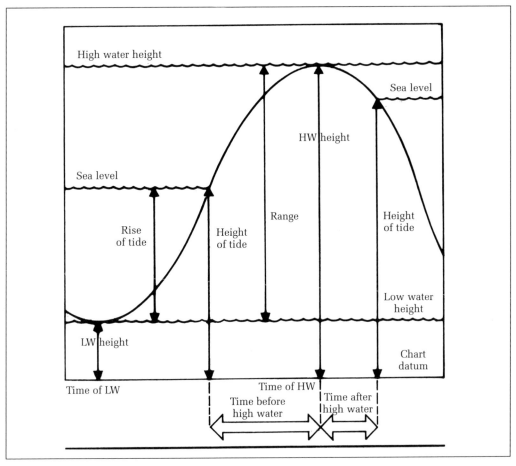

Fig 30   The tidal curve.

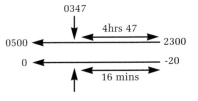

4 hours x 3.33   13.32
Plus 47 minutes (3.33 ÷ 60 x 47)   2.6
                = 15.92, call it 16 minutes.

That is 16 minutes away from −20 minutes, towards 00 minutes, leaving a correction of −04 minutes.

Differences Cowes

Portsmouth GMT	High Water	Low Water	BST Cowes
0347		−4	0443
1041	?		
1606		?	
2301	?		

Complete the other corrections yourself. Answers for this question (1) can be found at the end of the chapter.

Now turn your attention to the tidal height corrections. Remember you have worked out that it is a spring tide from the range.

We will expect to arrive in Cowes between 1130 and 1700

Tidal heights Portsmouth	Differences Cowes	Tidal heights Cowes
0.8	0.0	0.8
4.6	−0.5	4.1 ⎤
0.8	0.0	0.8 ⎦
4.7	−0.5	4.2

Set up the Cowes secondary port tidal curve as in Fig 31, to cover this bracket:

LW time 1703
LW height 0.8m
HW height 4.1m

When dealing with Solent ports, remember that the curves are unusual, in that they are worked around low water times.

You could save yourself time on the boat by carrying out any necessary calculations now, for the other places which you intend to visit.

Meteorological Information

There are plenty of sources of weather information. The nautical almanac will list many of them with broadcast times and frequencies. The Shipping Forecast, broadcast on Radio Four, will give gale warnings, the general synopsis, sea area forecasts and reports from coastal stations. The Inshore Waters Forecast, for UK waters up to twelve nautical miles offshore, will include the wind direction and strength, visibility and weather, followed by latest information from coastal stations when available.

Local Radio Stations broadcast a forecast for local coastal waters which can be useful. Marinecall is weather information by telephone. Current weather reports, two-day inshore forecasts and planning forecasts are all available. Metfax is weather information by FAX. There are many services available, including two-day inshore forecasts and charts, two- to five-day area planners and charts, satellite

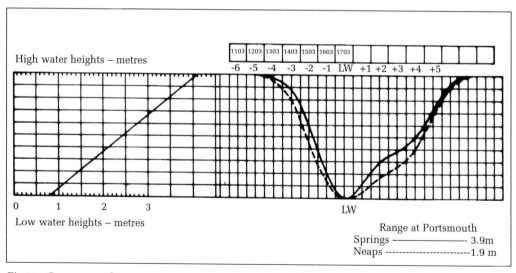

Fig 31   Cowes secondary port.

images, shipping forecasts, Beaufort scale, analysis charts and much more. For an index page of Metfax Marine, fax 0336 400401.

While you are at sea, you can continue to monitor the weather in many ways. The UK Coast Guard provides a regular four-hourly forecast. Strong wind or gale warnings are broadcast every two hours. UK Coast Radio Stations broadcast gale warnings, weather bulletins and weather forecasts. All forecasts are announced on VHF Channel 16 but broadcast on a working channel. Details of broadcast times can be obtained from nautical almanacs.

Navtex is an international automated system, broadcast on 518 kHz, containing navigational and weather information. Navtex units can be purchased at quite reasonable cost. They are a must for people hoping to venture to foreign waters, where information may not be as readily available as it is here. Reception range can be up to about 400 nautical miles from the transmitting station.

Other sources of information that tend to be overlooked are your own records and observations. It is worth learning some basic meteorology, enabling you to interpret the charts which are now readily available. Simple barometric trends and cloud formation can give you some general pointers as to how the weather systems are progressing.

The Beaufort Scale

Admiral Beaufort's wind speeds and associated sea states are relevant to open seas. It is important to remember that they do not take into account effects due to coastlines or any tide which may be running. On the Beaufort scale 17–21

knots of wind is classified as a fresh breeze. Over open waters this will generate a moderate sea state, that is waves of 1.25–2.5m. This is probably the maximum force to choose to be out in non-sheltered waters, in most mid-range motor boats. However, if an opposing tide is added to this wind force, you could expect to find a rough sea state (2.5–4m) with two knots, or very rough (4–6m) with five knots of foul tide. These variations should be taken into consideration when passage planning. Sea state is particularly important to you in a motor boat. You should try to arrange a wind with tide situation for your passage, giving a calmer sea state, whenever possible. In a fast motor boat, it is possible to outrun the tidal element when it is against you.

Weather Systems

Weather is caused by uneven heating of the surface of the earth. Wind flows from high to low pressure and is named after its direction of origin, i.e. Westerly winds come from the West. Atmospheric pressure is measured in millibars and isobars join points of equal pressure. The closer together the isobars, the stronger the winds will be. It is important to follow the weather for a few days before you go boating, to give you an overall picture of what is happening and what to expect.

Low Pressure System or Depression

Wind within a low pressure system in the northern hemisphere will revolve in an anticlockwise direction, with the wind being deflected slightly inwards towards the centre. A bird's eye view of a depression can be seen in Fig 32. Warm air, following the warm front, will have originated in the Azores and contains a lot of moisture. The heat in the air gives energy to the system. The warm air within the system is rising and therefore cooling. As warm moist air cools, it gives up its moisture, forming cloud. Cloud is therefore mainly concentrated around the cold and warm fronts. Fig 33 shows a section through a depression, with movement of air causing cloud and rain, which you would expect to see as it passes over you. The deeper the central pressure, the greater the ascent of air. The steeper the pressure gradients, the stronger the winds are likely to be. A deep low is therefore associated with extensive cloud, rain and strong winds. Once the cold front, which is travelling slightly faster, catches the warm front, they merge and form an occlusion. The source of warm air is then cut off and with it the source of energy. At this point the system starts to fill and die.

With the understanding of a few basic rules, it is straightforward to forecast the weather within a system. However, it is much more difficult to forecast where the system will track. Don't be too disheartened if things don't go according to your forecast as even the experts get it wrong from time to time. Most people will remember that we were assured there would not be hurricane force winds in 1987!

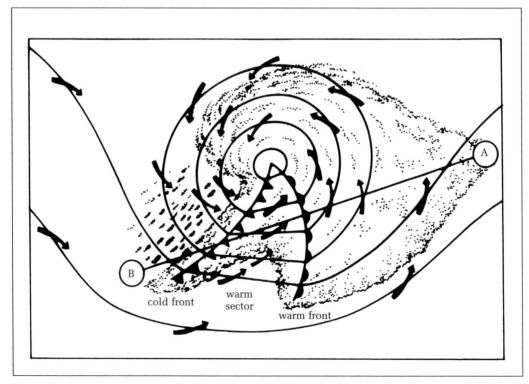

Fig 32   Bird's-eye view of a depression.

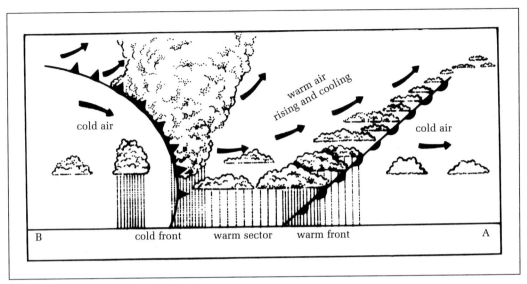

Fig 33   Section through a depression.

Facts About a Depression

- The central pressure will generally range from 950 to 1,015 mbs

- The diameter can range from 100–2000 nautical miles

- The surface winds will generally range from 10–70 knots

- The speed at which the system moves along its course is up to 70 knots

- Height of circular spiralling air can be up to 15km

- Of course there will always be exceptions.

Terms

There are many terms used in weather forecasts that have precise meanings. The more important ones are as follows:

Gale warnings:

Imminent	Within six hours of the time of issue
Soon	Six to twelve hours from the time of issue
Later	Beyond twelve hours from the time of issue

Beaufort force:

Light	Force 1–3
Moderate	Force 4
Fresh	Force 5
Strong	Force 6–7
Gale	Force 8

Visibility:

Good	More than five nautical miles.
Moderate	Two to five nautical miles.
Poor	1,000 metres to two nautical miles.
Fog	Less than 1,000 metres.

High Pressure Systems

High pressure systems tend to be associated with quiet, often fine weather giving warm sunny days in summer and cold frosty days in winter. In the northern hemisphere, the wind will revolve in a clockwise direction, being deflected slightly outwards from the centre. In these systems, cold dry air is falling and warming. In so doing, any cloud formation tends to evaporate and disperse. If cloud does persist, it is not very thick and can therefore only produce drizzle or very light rain. Pressure gradients are not usually very steep, so winds are often light, unless there is a squeeze being produced by an adjacent low pressure system. There are no fronts associated with high pressure systems.

Sea Breeze

On a sunny day, the land will heat up, the warm air will rise and cause an area of low pressure over land near the coast. Cold air is sucked in from over the sea to replace it as you will see in Fig 34. As the system builds, its influence moves further out to sea, sometimes tens of miles. The wind speeds will increase towards the land and can be Force 3–4 by mid afternoon. If the gradient wind is onshore, the sea breeze is less likely to form. When passage planning, if your trip takes you inshore late on a sunny afternoon, bear in

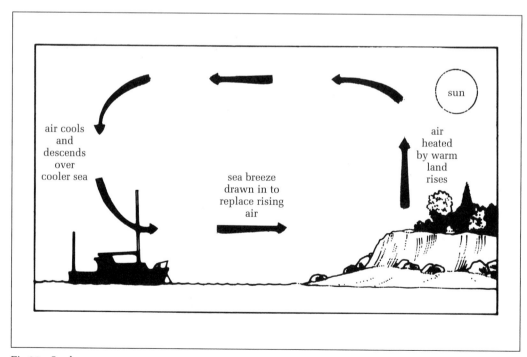

Fig 34   Sea breeze.

mind that the closer in you get, the stronger the sea breeze could become.

Land Breeze

At night the land begins to cool quickly, but the sea holds its heat. An opposite system starts to build. By 1800 hrs the sea breeze is dying and an offshore wind may be in force by around 2200 hrs. Land breezes are much weaker than sea breezes.

Fog

Advection fog is caused by warm moist air flowing over a cold sea. As the air cools, it gives up its moisture, and forms fog. It is possible to get quite strong wind with this type of fog. The Channel Islands are often badly affected, with deep cold water and warm southerly winds.

Radiation fog is caused by cooling of the ground at night after a relatively warm day. When the ground cools it cools the air above it, causing it to give up its moisture and form fog. Often this fog drifts out to sea, maybe up to as much as ten miles offshore. If the sea is relatively warm, the fog is gradually dispersed. The sun will tend to burn off any remaining fog in the morning.

Winds

Gradient winds follow a set pattern around a weather system. However, they are affected when they come into contact with land. Winds can be deflected around headlands and become much more gusty. Keep well clear of a lee shore, that is one where the wind is blowing directly on to land. If the sea bed shelves to the shore, strong winds will cause waves to break.

Any harbour with its entrance or approach open to windward can quickly become hazardous in strong wind conditions. It could be better to stay at sea under these circumstances if no alternative shelter is available – not an easy decision for the skipper of a small boat to make, with night approaching and a tired, cold and seasick crew threatening mutiny! It is better to predict the weather and not get into this situation.

Having watched the weather for a few days, you should have a better idea of the established pattern and know what to expect for your passage. Never be afraid to change your mind. If the family is set on a weekend in Weymouth leaving from the Hamble and Westerly force 6 is forecast, the responsible skipper will decide to spend the weekend in the Solent. If the said skipper is very inexperienced, he may even decide to spend the weekend gardening! There is absolutely nothing wrong with that. Never let yourself be pressured into a situation with which you are uncomfortable.

Summary

It is advisable to do as much preparation as you can in advance. There are three reasons for doing this. First, you have a clearer picture of the expected weather patterns and can better predict the weather for your passage. Secondly, if you have planned in an organized way you are unlikely to leave without something of importance. The third reason is that if you prepare your passage in advance, the time that you are actually onboard can be spent cruising and enjoying yourself.

Questions

1 Tidal height questions posed in text (in Tidal Information section).
2 What useful passage planning information can be obtained from a navigation chart?
3 For what period of time would you use tidal stream information for a high water at 1448 hrs?
4 Look at the diagram of a low pressure system. If you were in position A, describe the weather you would expect to experience as the system passes overhead.
5 If you were in the Western Solent, in a small motor boat, and heard Southerly gale force 8 imminent, would you start a passage to Brighton?

Answers

1 Second low water 1606, falls within 1100 to 1700 band, again moving from -20 minutes to 00 minutes.
Our correction is 5 hours 6 mins. 5 x 3.33 + 0.34 = 16.99, call it 17 minutes. That is 17 minutes away from -20 minutes, towards 00 minutes, leaving a correction of −03 minutes.
First high water 1041 GMT, falls between 0600 and 1200, moving from +15 minutes towards −15 minutes. This is a six hour band with each hour worth 5 minutes.

0000 0600
1200 1800

−0015 +0015

Our correction is 4 hrs 41 mins. 4 x 5 + 3.42 = 23.42 mins, call it 24 minutes. That is 24 minutes away from +15, towards −15, leaving a correction of −9 minutes.
Second high water 2301 GMT, falls between 1800 and 0000, moving again from +15 to −15 minutes. Your correction

is 5 hours 1 minute. 5 x 5 = 25 minutes, leaving a correction of −10 minutes.

Differences Cowes

Portsmouth GMT	High Water	Low Water	BST Cowes
0347		−4	0443
1041	-9		1132
1606		−3	1703
2301	-10		2351

2 You need to look at the chart for any tidal races, bolt holes, shallow water areas or bars. Note any conspicuous objects such as lighthouses, racons, etc. Buoys, leading lines or marks can be identified for your pilotage notes.
3 You would use this information from 1418 hrs until 1518 hrs.
4 The arrival of a low pressure system will be indicated by high cirrus cloud and a watery sun. Barometric pressure will start to fall slowly. As the warm front approaches, winds will back slightly from SSW to S. Cloud will become lower and thicker. Pressure will fall more quickly because the isobars are closer together. As the warm front passes, rain will start and visibility deteriorate. Winds will veer to SW. In the warm sector there will be drizzle, low cloud, a rise in temperature and fairly steady pressure. Passage of the cold front will bring more rain, which may be heavy. The temperature will fall again and there will be a quick rise in pressure. Winds will veer to NW and may be gusty. Visibility will improve as the front passes. There may be showers after the front, or occasionally thunder storms.
5 No, if there is a gale imminent from the South, within the next six hours, a passage in unsheltered waters, along a lee shore, with your destination being open to the South could be very dangerous.

6

THE INTERNATIONAL REGULATIONS FOR PREVENTING COLLISIONS AT SEA

The International Regulations for Preventing Collisions at Sea are the nautical equivalent of the Highway Code. They are written in legalese but you are not required to quote them word for word or by number. However, it is very important to have a working knowledge of the meaning of these regulations as they are legally binding and apply to all vessels on the high seas and connected waters. Day Skippers are required to study rules 5, 7–10 and 12–19 in particular.

The steering and sailing rules are divided into three sections. The conduct of vessels in any condition of visibility is covered by rules 4–10, that of vessels in sight of one another by rules 11–18 and the conduct of vessels in restricted visibility by rule 19.

Conduct of Vessels in any Condition of Visibility
(Steering and sailing rules, Section I)

Lookout

Rule 5 is the most important one. It requires every vessel to maintain a proper lookout at all times, by sight, hearing and any other available means appropriate. If you are not keeping a good lookout, the remaining rules become academic. As already mentioned, blind areas can be a hazard when driving from the inside helm position, so check them regularly or, better still, post a lookout. Looking behind is often neglected in a fast motor boat because you are travelling at speed. However, there is often someone who can travel faster, so look out for them. Awareness of others is a very important quality for a skipper to develop. If you use radar, you should be aware of its limitations. It is possible to misinterpret a radar picture – you may have heard of radar-assisted collisions!

Safe Speed

You are required, by rule 6, to proceed at a safe speed. What constitutes a safe speed will differ from one situation to another and does require a modicum of common sense. When determining a safe speed, take into account the state of visibility, proximity of navigational hazards and the number of other vessels in the area. Also consider the sea state and your ability to manoeuvre your vessel. Always be prepared for sailing yachts tacking in front of you. Remember that they cannot move directly into the wind like you can. They have to tack backwards

Always be prepared for sailing yachts tacking in front of you.

and forwards and their draught may be greater than yours, so they may require deeper water. When travelling at speed, always be aware of the possible consequences of your wash. If you pass close to small boats, you run the risk of swamping them. Give them a wide berth and slow down if necessary.

The same consideration should be shown to the environment. Speed limits exist on most rivers for this very reason. If you create a lot of wash, you can destroy river banks and could also flood the nests of birds, especially those that are rare and endangered.

The picture changes at night and background lights can create a very confusing picture. You could think you had found a north cardinal mark, only to discover that it was a car's headlights flashing between trees ashore. Slowing down will give more time for interpretation.

Determining Risk of Collision

Rule 7 requires you to use all available means to determine whether or not a risk of collision exists. One way to determine risk is to take compass bearings of the other vessel. If the bearing does not appreciably change as range decreases, then risk of collision does exist. Once you have established that a danger exists, you then have to identify which of you is the give-way vessel. This is dealt with by rules 12, 13, 14, 15 and 18. However, rule 8 applies to all give-way vessels and requires avoiding action to be taken early, to be positive and taken with due regard to 'good seamanship'. This last phrase is included to remind you that you must be careful not to cause a second close-quarters situation by the action you take in avoiding the first. You should always avoid crossing ahead of a vessel to which you are giving way.

Narrow Channels

When you are proceeding down a narrow channel, rule 9 requires you to stay as near to the starboard side as is safe and practicable. If your vessel is less than 20 metres long you must also keep clear of large vessels that can only navigate safely within this channel. You should never anchor unless you have an emergency. If another vessel is on the wrong side of the channel and approaches you head-on, we would advise you to stop, rather than

Keep as near to the starboard side of a channel as is safe and practicable. Sometimes withies are used to mark the channel.

You are on the correct side of the channel. If there is insufficient draught for you to go outside the buoys, your only safe option is to sound the 'wake up' signal, five short blasts, followed by three short blasts, 'I am operating astern propulsion', and stop your vessel. Avoid altering course to port.

incorrectly altering course to port. It is possible that the skipper of the other vessel has gone below and an inexperienced helmsman has been left in charge. If the skipper comes back on deck and suddenly but correctly alters course to starboard, just as you alter course to port, you will be in the wrong if you collide. If there is insufficient draught for you to go outside the buoys, your only safe option is to sound the 'wake up' signal, five short blasts, followed by three short blasts, 'I am operating astern propulsion', and stop your vessel.

Traffic Separation Schemes

Traffic separation schemes are made up of two lanes divided by a separation zone. They are shown on Admiralty charts in magenta. Rule 10 requires a vessel using a scheme to proceed in the appropriate lane, joining and leaving at the ends if possible. However, if you must join in the middle, do so at as narrow an angle to the general flow as possible, in the same way that you would use a slip road in your car. Avoid anchoring near a separation scheme and if your vessel is less than 20 metres long, you must not impede a power-driven vessel which is navigating within the scheme. If you are intending to cross a traffic lane, you must use a heading (not a ground track) which is at right angles to the general traffic flow. This will be apparent to large ships monitoring your progress by radar and perhaps by shore stations such as Dover Coastguard, who keep a radar watch over the Dover Strait Traffic Separation Scheme.

Conduct of Vessels in Sight of One Another
(Steering and sailing rules, Section II)

The rules define a give-way vessel and a stand-on vessel.

Identifying the Give-Way Vessel

A power-driven vessel must give way to just about everybody! Vessels not under command, vessels restricted in their ability to manoeuvre, vessels constrained by their draught, vessels engaged in fishing and sailing vessels.

Any vessel overtaking another vessel and approaching within the sector of the stern light must keep out of the way of the vessel being overtaken. This is rule 13 and applies whatever the types of vessel concerned.

Rule 14 states that if two power-driven vessels are motoring head-on towards each other, they must both give way and alter course to starboard. In this case at night, you would see each other's port and starboard side-lights and masthead light.

If another motor boat is approaching on your starboard side you must give way. Imagine that at night you would see the other vessel's port navigation light, then the rhyme 'If to starboard red appears, 'tis your duty to keep clear', might help you to remember. This is rule 15 and applies to vessels approaching in the sector that would be covered by your green navigation light.

Conduct of sailing vessels is covered by rule 12. Although they do not apply to you, you should have a knowledge of them. If there are two sailing vessels ahead of you, you must know which will give way to the other as it might influence the action you take yourself. If two sailing vessels are on opposite tacks, the one on port tack (that is the one with the mainsail over the starboard side of the boat) is the give-way vessel. If two sailing vessels are on the same tack, the windward boat is the give-way vessel. If a sailing vessel is on port tack and she cannot determine the tack of a windward vessel, she will give way.

Give-Way and Stand-On Vessels

Now that you have decided which is the give-way vessel the other must be the stand-on vessel and the actions of each are covered by Rules 16 and 17. As give-way vessel, you are required to take positive, substantial action in good time. At night, substantial action means a sufficiently large alteration of course to show a different aspect of your navigation lights to the other vessel. When giving way, think of all the considerations you had when determining a safe speed – are there any navigational hazards, or will you cause a risk of collision with another vessel by avoiding this one?

As stand-on vessel you are required to maintain your course and speed. However, rule 17(a)(ii) exists to relieve you from having to 'play chicken' with the skipper who does not know of the existence of the rules, or thinks they apply to everyone else but him. If it becomes obvious that the give-way vessel is not going to abide by the rules, you may take avoiding action yourself. You must take avoiding action if it becomes obvious that without your action a collision will result.

Conduct of Vessels in Restricted Visibility
(Steering and sailing rules, Section III)

It is important to understand that the collision regulations change radically for vessels not in sight of one another due to restricted visibility. None of the rules in Section II apply. No vessel has right of way and no vessel is the stand-on vessel. Rule 19 tells us that all vessels must determine if a close-quarters situation or risk of collision is developing, and if so, shall take avoiding action in ample time. The rule goes on to give the following advice on what action to take. If a risk of collision is detected by radar alone, avoid

an alteration of course to port for a vessel forward of your beam and an alteration of course towards a vessel abeam or aft of the beam. Furthermore, rule 19 states that every vessel shall proceed at a safe speed and give due consideration to the prevailing circumstances, when complying with rules which apply to vessels in any condition of visibility – that is, the rules contained in Section I. Rule 19 concludes with the following requirement: on hearing a fog signal forward of your beam, reduce speed to a minimum to maintain steerage and navigate with extreme caution.

You should do as much as you can to reduce the risk of being run down in fog. Use a radar reflector, keep a good lookout and listening watch. The crew member with the best hearing should be given this job, preferably outside and as far away from the engines as possible. Sound your appropriate fog signals. Give the fog horn to the person who can switch off their hearing aid! Be ready to take immediate avoiding action and keep clear of shipping channels. You will be far safer in shallow water.

Additional Rules

Manoeuvring Signals

The manoeuvring signals which you should know are included in Rule 34 and only apply to power-driven vessels in sight of one another. One short blast means that the vessel is altering course to starboard. Two short blasts mean the vessel is altering course to port. Three short blasts mean that the vessel is operating astern propulsion. This does not necessarily mean that the vessel is

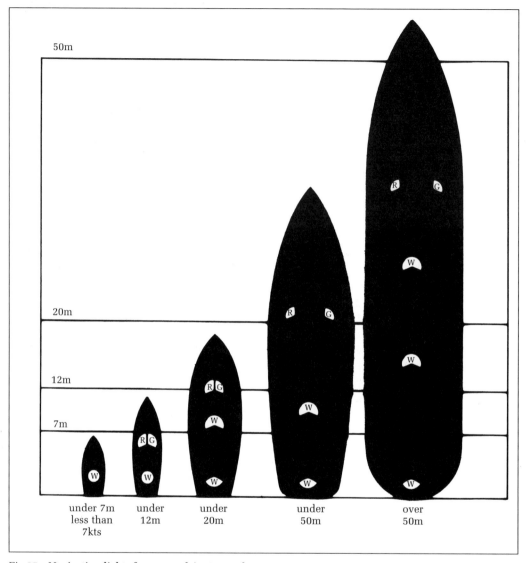

Fig 35   **Navigation lights for power-driven vessels.**

moving astern, it may simply be slowing down. Five or more short and rapid blasts mean 'wake up', the vessel does not understand your intentions, or is in doubt that you are taking sufficient action to avoid a collision.

Lights and Shapes

Light requirements for power-driven vessels under way are specified in rule 23 and shown in Fig 35. Lights for other vessels are covered by rules 24–30 and sound signals for vessels in restricted visibility by rule 35.

A power-driven vessel less than 7 metres in length whose speed does not exceed 7 knots may combine the masthead and stern light in an all-round white light and, if practicable, show sidelights.

A power-driven vessel less than 12 metres in length may combine the masthead and stern light in an all-round white light displaced from the centre line, if fitting on the centre line is not practicable. However, the sidelights should be combined in one lantern carried on the centre line.

A power-driven vessel less than 20 metres in length must have a separate masthead light and stern light, but may combine the sidelights in one lantern carried on the centre line.

A power-driven vessel over 50 metres in length must show two masthead lights, the aft one higher than the forward one, a stern light and separate sidelights. Vessels less than 50 metres in length need show only one masthead light.

Vessels under sail are required to carry only sidelights and a stern light. Yachts under 20 metres may combine these lights in a single lantern at the masthead. When under power, they must show the lights prescribed above for a power-driven vessel.

You should also be able to recognise the sound signals, lights and day shapes of pilot vessels, vessels not under command, restricted in their ability to manoeuvre, fishing, trawling and dredging.

Power-Driven Vessel

A power-driven vessel shall exhibit the standard navigation lights described above, according to its length.

Power-driven vessel less than 50 metres, under way and making way.

SOUND SIGNAL   One long blast every two minutes.
Power-driven vessel under way but stopped.
SOUND SIGNAL   Two long blasts every two minutes.

Pilot Vessel

A pilot vessel on duty shall exhibit all round white and red lights in a vertical line, 'white hats and red noses' may help you remember. In addition, when under way, she shall show sidelights and a stern light. If the vessel is not being used for pilot duty, she shall show the lights appropriate to a vessel of her length.

Pilot vessel at work.

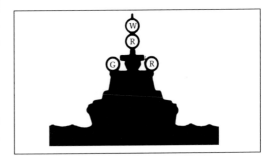

SOUND SIGNAL   As above, followed by four short blasts.

Sailing Vessels

A sailing vessel shall exhibit the standard navigation lights described above, according to its length.

Sailing vessel under way.

SOUND SIGNAL   One long and two short blasts every two minutes.
DAY SHAPE   Black cone apex pointing down, if motoring with sails hoisted.

Towing

A vessel towing shall exhibit two masthead lights forward when the length of the tow measures less than 200 metres and three masthead lights forward if the tow exceeds this length. In addition, it shall show sidelights, a stern light and a yellow towing light in a vertical line above the stern light. The vessel being towed shall exhibit sidelights and a stern light.

Tug less than 50 metres and tow over 200 metres.

See below.
SOUND SIGNAL FOR TUG   One long and two short blasts every two minutes.
SOUND SIGNAL FOR TOW   One long and three short blasts every two minutes.
DAY SHAPE   Black diamond on both.

Fishing Vessels

Vessels trawling shall exhibit all-round green and white lights in a vertical line. In addition, a vessel over 50 metres shall exhibit a masthead light abaft and higher than the green all-round light. Vessels engaged in fishing shall exhibit all-round red and white lights in a vertical line. In addition, all vessels when making way shall exhibit sidelights and a stern light. If the vessel is not being used for fishing or trawling, she shall show the lights appropriate to a vessel of her length.

Note that the fishing vessel over 50m

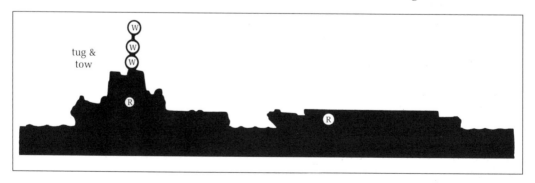

does not show a second, higher masthead light, as this could be confused with the lights of a pilot vessel on duty.

Fishing vessel fishing.

SOUND SIGNAL One long and two short blasts every two minutes.
DAY SHAPE Two cones apexes together.

Trawler less than 50 metres trawling.

SOUND SIGNAL One long and two short blasts every two minutes.
DAY SHAPE Two cones apexes together.

Under the pre-1995 regulations, fishing vessels and trawlers under 20 metres could show the alternative day shape of a basket instead of the cones. Amendments

in 1995 removed this concession, but you are still likely to see vessels displaying baskets.

Vessel Restricted in its Ability to Manoeuvre

A vessel restricted in its ability to manoeuvre shall exhibit all-round red, white and red lights in a vertical line. In addition, when making way the vessel shall exhibit masthead light/s, sidelights and a stern light.

Vessel probably over 50 metres, restricted in its ability to manoeuvre.

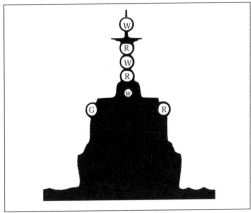

SOUND SIGNAL One long and two short blasts every two minutes.
DAY SHAPE Ball, diamond, ball in a vertical line.

Vessel Constrained by its Draught

A vessel constrained by its draught shall exhibit three all-round red lights in a vertical line. In addition, when under way she shall exhibit a masthead light/s, sidelights and a stern light.

Vessel less than 50 metres, constrained by its draught.

SOUND SIGNAL One long and two short blasts every two minutes.
DAY SHAPE A cylinder.

Vessel Not Under Command

A vessel not under command shall exhibit two all round red lights in a vertical line, plus side lights and stern light if making way.

Vessel not under command, making way.

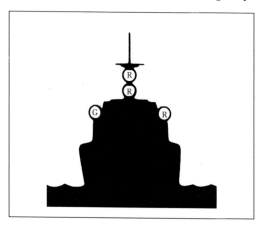

SOUND SIGNAL One long and two short blasts every two minutes.
DAY SHAPE Two black balls.

Dredger

A vessel engaged in dredging will be restricted in her ability to manoeuvre and shall show the appropriate lights. In addition, she shall exhibit two all-round red lights on the obstructed side and two all-round green lights on the clear side.

A dredger dredging.

SOUND SIGNAL One long and two short blasts every two minutes.

DAY SHAPE Two black balls on obstructed side. Two diamonds on clear side and a ball, diamond, ball in a vertical line.

Vessels Engaged in Diving

If a vessel is engaged in diving operations, she shall show the lights for a vessel restricted in her ability to manoeuvre with an obstructed side as above. Small vessels engaged in diving may exhibit a metre-high rigid replica of the international code flag 'A' instead.

SHORT AND LONG BLASTS

The term 'short blast' means a blast of about one second's duration. The term 'long blast' means a blast of from four to six seconds' duration.

Distress Signals

Lastly, the regulations list fifteen ways of indicating distress.

In coastal waters, you would probably choose:

1 Mayday by radiotelephony.
2 Red rocket parachute or hand flare.
3 Orange smoke signal.
4 Flames on the vessel. Most of us do not go to sea with the infamous barrel of tar; however, if your vessel was on fire, this in itself would indicate distress.

In addition, you may possibly have:

5 International code signal of N and C flags.
6 A square flag and a ball.

Small craft with less safety gear might consider:

7 Continuous sounding of a fog horn.
8 Slowly and repeatedly raising and lowering of outstretched arms.

In addition, large craft or vessels venturing further afield may have:

9 Emergency Position-Indicating Radio Beacons: EPIRBs.
10 Rockets or shells, throwing red stars one at a time at short intervals.
11 The morse code . . . – – – . . . SOS.
12 Radiotelegraph alarm signal.
13 Radiotelephone alarm signal.
14 Approved signals transmitted by radio communication systems.

15 A gun or similar, fired at one minute intervals.

Summary

These regulations are very important and form the basis of safety at sea. You will probably have witnessed the chaos caused by someone instinctively driving on the wrong side of the road when abroad. In this country we can still buy a vessel and take it to sea with no knowledge or previous experience. However, we feel that you have a responsibility to take care of your crew and not to endanger or inconvenience other boaters.

Questions

1 You are the skipper of vessel A in each of the pictures in Fig 37. What action would you take in each situation and why?
2 Should you sound manoeuvring signals if you are in fog and other vessels are only detectable by radar or sound?
3 Name four ways of indicating distress, which you might choose to use in coastal waters.

Answers

1a You are the give-way vessel. Make a substantial alteration of course to starboard and pass astern of vessel B. Continue to monitor the vessel until she is past and clear.
1b You are both the give-way vessel and should both alter course to starboard.
1c You are the overtaking vessel, keep your distance until you are past and clear. There is no recommended side or distance to pass in the regulations. However, since the sailing vessel is on starboard tack, it would be kinder to pass on her port side to avoid disturbing her wind. Out of courtesy, we recommend a minimum passing distance of 50 metres for reasons of wash.

1d   You are on the correct side of the channel. Ideally, if there is sufficient room between vessel B and the green buoys, alter course to starboard as for a head-on situation. If not and there is insufficient draught for you to go outside the buoys, your only safe option is to sound the 'wake up' signal, five short blasts, followed by three short blasts, 'I am operating astern propulsion', and stop your vessel. On no account make an incorrect manoeuvre to port.

1e   You are **required** under rule 17 to keep your course and speed as stand-on vessel. If at any time you feel that a collision could not be avoided by the give-way vessel alone, you are **required** to take avoiding action. However, you **may** take action to avoid collision by your manoeuvre alone as soon as it becomes apparent that the other vessel is not taking action. In this case, you might decide to take the action yourself as she is a large vessel and you may consider it courteous to avoid putting her to the trouble of altering course. You must, however, ensure that you take this action well in advance. A serious reduction in speed, say to 50 per cent, is probably your best option.

1f   This vessel is flying flag Alpha, so you will know that there may be divers in the water. Pass at a substantial distance and reduce your speed.

2   No, they only apply to vessels in sight of one another. You should sound your appropriate fog signal.

3   In coastal waters, you would probably choose a Mayday message by radiotelephony, red parachute or hand flares, orange smoke signal, or if your vessel is on fire, there may be flames visible.

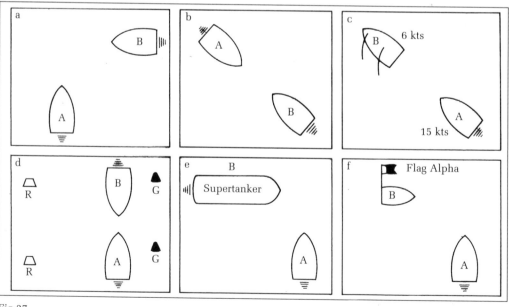

Fig 37.

7

LEAVING YOUR BERTH

The day has arrived, hopefully along with the sunshine and light winds! All of your planning and checks are complete and your safety brief has been delivered. Now you have to stow your gear, consider last-minute navigation and make a plan for leaving your berth.

Stowing Gear

Personal gear and victuals have to be stowed in a way that will not cause harm or annoyance. There is a lot of psychology to consider when you are boating. In effect you are putting people in a confined space and taking them to sea, from where there is no escape. It can be compared with putting someone in prison, except that the prisoner could be given more room! We all have our territorial space around us, which will be greater with some people than others and we become uncomfortable if people enter this space uninvited.

Some of your guests will be very untidy and want to leave their personal possessions scattered all over the boat, even over somebody else's bunk. This can cause much annoyance to some people over a period of time, so make a rule whenever a new crew member comes onboard. Allocate them a space of their own for their gear, encourage them to use it and other crew members to respect it. Victuals should be stowed in a communal space so that everyone can take a turn at preparing food and drinks. Try to avoid stowing items in areas which will become unstable in rough conditions. Nothing will stay where you put it when under way, unless it is captive. If you leave a cup of coffee on a table, do not expect it to be there when you come back. There is nothing worse than going down below after a rough trip to find unnecessary damage and breakages. Finally, make sure that doors and hatches are properly secured and the gas has been turned off.

Navigation

Take the chart on which you drew your intended route. Assuming that you are still happy with your chosen destination, decide on a departure time from your present position. Turn to the tidal stream information which you have already marked up for the day and make a note of the direction and rate of the tide for the duration of your passage. You will have noted that for our fictitious passage there are spring tides. Therefore take the larger

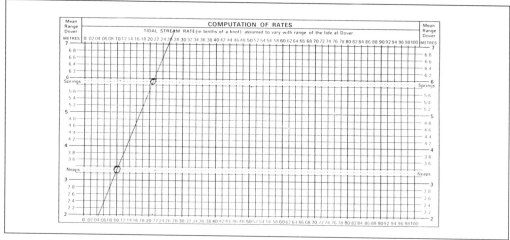

Fig 38.

number as the rate, if you are using a tidal stream atlas. For example, if the rate is listed as 10,21 it indicates a mean neap rate of 1.0 knot and a mean spring rate of 2.1 knots. The comma indicates the approximate position at which the information was obtained. You would use 2.1 knots as the rate for this particular day, because it is a spring tide. The direction can be established using a Breton plotter or similar.

If you are between spring and neap tides, you would use the 'computation of rates' table as in Fig 38. For this particular example, you would put a circle around the 1.0 on the neaps row of dots and another around the 2.1 on the springs row of dots. Join the two dots with a pencil line and extend the line to the scale at the top and bottom. Work out the range at the standard port for the required day and mark it on the left scale. Follow this line across to where it intersects the diagonal line and read up or down to the scale to

If the tide is going to have an effect on you, construct a tidal vector.

find the rate. If using tidal diamonds on a chart, the rate and direction will be given on the chart itself in table form. The 'computation of rates' table can still be used if you are between spring and neap tides.

If the tide is going to have an effect on you, construct tidal vectors on the chart to compensate for it. Read through your 'Skipper's Notebook' to remind yourself of any relevant local information. When you feel that everything is ready, instruct your crew to single up the bow and stern lines and, if necessary, adjust the fenders for departure.

Warps and Fenders

A fore spring prevents the boat moving forward and a back spring prevents the boat moving backward. Providing there is no adverse wind or tide to consider, you can remove the springs. The stern line is now singled up, ready to slip from onboard and one crew member can be in charge of it. Do this by first removing the turns from the cleat onboard; however, do not remove the end which is attaching the warp to the boat. Remove the turns from the pontoon cleat next, but leave a loop around it. Take care not to lose control of the boat at this stage.

Take up the slack and put a turn or two around the onboard cleat again, so that the weight of the boat is not being held in your crew member's hand. It is very important to take these turns, otherwise when you start to manoeuvre on the bow line, your crew will not be able to hold the line and they could be injured. If you have very long warps, adjust them, so that your crew is left with only a short length to release. If you have 10 metres of rope to pull round the cleat, there is more risk of a tangle and a jam. Do the same with the bow line and put someone in charge of that as well if you have enough crew.

Adjust your fenders, ensuring that there are two or three on the bow, providing the hull with protection at pontoon height. If you are in a tight spot, with another vessel moored close by, put fenders on the other side of your boat at a suitable height. If you have plenty of crew members, one could carry a fender and act as a 'roving fender'. Check that there are no warps hanging over the side near

A fore spring prevents the boat moving forward and a back spring prevents the boat moving backward.

the propellers and start the engines. Make sure that you have oil pressure and that water is exiting from the exhausts if you have inboard engines. At this stage, everybody can get onboard and guard rails may be secured. Make an entry in your ship's log of time, barometric pressure, log reading, wind direction with force and bilge pump run, along with any remarks.

Leaving a Pontoon (Shaft Drive)

Test your engine controls by going gently ahead and astern on each one. The bow and stern ropes will stop the boat going anywhere and there should still be a few turns on the cleats to stop the crew members feeling any strain on the warps. Next, put your outside engine in tickover astern. Paddle wheel effect will push the vessel on to the pontoon and you can give the order to 'let go aft'. If you only have one crew member onboard, put a lock on

the bow line and leave it while dealing with the stern line. Now look around and make sure that your exit is clear, engage the inside engine astern then take the outside engine out of gear. Paddle wheel effect will now take the stern of the vessel away from the pontoon (Fig 39). The bow will swing in, which is why it was important to fender it. You can swing out on the bow line as far as you like at this point. If you are on a hammer head, you might like to swing out to 45° or more. However, if you are in a finger berth, your swing will be limited by an adjacent boat or pontoon. As mentioned before, you are never committed to a manoeuvre until you release the bow line. If you change your mind at any time, you can simply put the outside engine astern and take the inside engine out of gear and move gently back against the pontoon.

Try to have an engine in gear at all times when carrying out this manoeuvre, to avoid allowing the bow line to slacken and the vessel to drift forward. Once you are happy with your position, instruct

Engage the inside engine astern to swing away from the pontoon.

When you are ready, instruct your crew to 'let go forward'.

your crew to 'let go forward'. Put both engines into neutral for a moment to take the tension off while your crew releases the bow rope and pulls it back onboard. When your crew member advises you that your bow line is 'clear', put both engines astern and pull away.

In fresh conditions, if you are being blown on to the pontoon, you may need to engage the outside engine ahead at fewer revs than the inside engine. Turn the wheel towards the pontoon to help the swing away. In this case, when you drop the engines out of gear also return the helm to midships.

If you are being blown away from the pontoon, you may only need to release your warps and let the wind do the job for you.

Heavy displacement vessels will

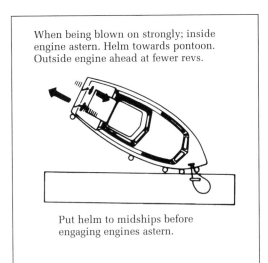

When being blown on strongly; inside engine astern. Helm towards pontoon. Outside engine ahead at fewer revs.

Put helm to midships before engaging engines astern.

Fig 39(b)   **Shaft drive when being blown on strongly.**

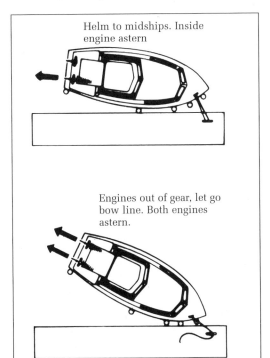

Helm to midships. Inside engine astern

Engines out of gear, let go bow line. Both engines astern.

Fig 39(a)   **Shaft drive.**

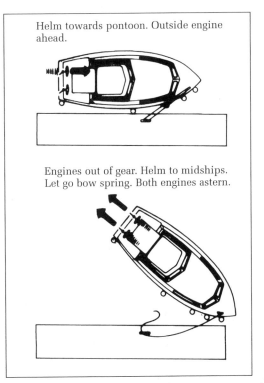

Helm towards pontoon. Outside engine ahead.

Engines out of gear. Helm to midships. Let go bow spring. Both engines astern.

Fig 39(c)   **Shaft drive using a spring.**

probably respond more successfully to the use of a spring, in place of a bow line. Rig the warp from the bow of your vessel to a cleat on the pontoon amidships. Engage the outside engine ahead to produce the same effect as before. The stern will swing away from the pontoon and the bows will swing in, on to the fenders. The spring will check any forward motion of the boat. Using a spring has a much stronger effect than using a bow line and is not recommended for light displacement vessels unless the conditions are really brisk (see Fig 39).

Leaving a Pontoon (Outdrive)

Make your checks and rig warps and fenders the same as for shaft drive boats. Put the outside engine astern; if the conditions are fresh you may need to turn the wheel towards the pontoon in order to hold the boat alongside. Slip the stern line and gently turn your wheel away. In light airs, this may be enough to bring the stern away from the pontoon. However, if you need a greater effect, engage the inside engine astern as well, to swing the stern away from the pontoon. When you have enough angle between yourself and the pontoon, take the engine(s) out of gear, release the bow line, put the helm to midships and engage both engines astern to pull away.

In fresh conditions, if you are being blown on to the pontoon, you may need to rig a spring, turn your wheel towards the pontoon and put your outside engine ahead to pull you off. Again, take the engine out of gear, release the bow line, put the helm to midships and engage both engines astern to pull away (see Fig 40).

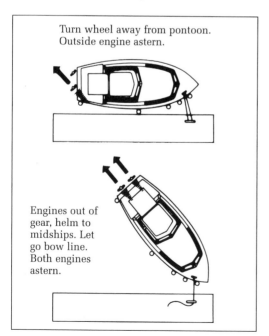

Turn wheel away from pontoon. Outside engine astern.

Engines out of gear, helm to midships. Let go bow line. Both engines astern.

Fig 40(a)   **Outdrive.**

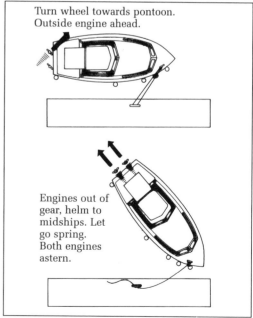

Turn wheel towards pontoon. Outside engine ahead.

Engines out of gear, helm to midships. Let go spring. Both engines astern.

Fig 40(b)   **Outdrive using a spring.**

Leaving the Marina and Putting to Sea

Once you are clear of your berth, request that warps and fenders are stowed. Warps should be coiled and stowed ready for their next use. Fenders should be removed and stowed in lockers or fender baskets. It is poor seamanship to leave fenders hanging over the side of your boat when under way.

Call the marina office on your VHF radio. Calling arrangements will be found in nautical almanacs. Most marinas should be called direct on their working channels. Advise them that you have left your berth and when you plan to return. Not all marinas require you to do this but we recommend it for two reasons. First, it checks your radio to ensure that it is working correctly. Observing this simple procedure could remove a great workload from the Coast Guard, who is always pleased to give you a 'radio check' if you are worried about your transmissions. With modern synthesized radios, however, if you can contact the marina on, say, channel 80, then almost certainly it will work on channel 16. Secondly, it is courteous and sets a precedent. If you always call every time you leave your berth and one day the vessel leaves with no call, the marina staff might look more carefully at the skipper, in case it is not you!

For your example you are leaving the Hamble River on passage to Cowes. Keep as near to the starboard side of the river as is safe and practicable and maintain a good lookout. Have your pilotage notes to hand. As you leave, you may work on a back bearing, as well as following a sketch which you have drawn in your 'Skipper's

Call the marina office by VHF radio on their working channel.

Notebook', perhaps ticking off the piles as you pass. If you were to undertake this passage at night, you would notice that there are two sets of leading lights to bring you safely into or out of the river. It is important to stay within the channel, as there are drying banks to either side. If the tide is running strongly, keep a lookout behind to ensure that you are not being pushed outside the piles. Once you reach Hamble Point South Cardinal Buoy, you can increase your speed, providing it is prudent to do so, and start your passage to Cowes.

Skipper's Notes for Hamble

Shelter Excellent.

Hazards Crowded river, unlit piles and buoys a danger at night, dries either side of the channel entrance.

Navigation Leading lights 345° on West shore. Front Oc (2) R 12s 4m 2M (no.

View across Southampton Water to Calshot from the River Hamble. This is a busy area for large shipping.

6 pile). Rear Q R 12m, 820m from front. Visible 341°–349°.

Second set of leading lights 026° on East shore. Front Q G (pile). Rear Iso G 6s.

VHF Hamble Harbour Radio Ch 68. Marinas use Ch 80.

Moorings Visitors buoys, piles, public pontoons and many marinas.

Facilities There is fuel available and a variety of yacht clubs.

Summary

Having done the bulk of your passage planning at home, there are only last-minute tidal stream calculations to do on the day. Give your crew members their own personal space if possible, no matter how small. Rig your fenders so that you have protection on the bows and on the other side of your vessel if there are craft nearby. Manoeuvre your vessel on a bow line for planing boats or a spring if you have a heavy displacement boat. Remember that you can change your mind at

any time until you let go of the bow line or spring. Communicate with your crew as in 'let go aft' and have them respond to you, as in 'clear' when they have carried out your instructions. These simple short commands ensure that everybody knows what is happening and mistakes are less likely to be made.

Questions

1 If it was spring tides and you saw 10,21 listed in a tidal stream atlas, which rate would you use?
2 What function do the 'springs' perform when a boat is moored up?
3 Why is it important to make sure that you have two or three fenders on the bow when manoeuvring?
4 Why is it important to have an engine in gear at all times when manoeuvring on a bow line?
5 Why would you bother to call the marina office and tell them that you were leaving your berth?

Answers

1 You would use 2 .1 knots as the rate for spring tides.
2 A fore spring prevents the boat moving forward and a back spring prevents the boat moving backward.
3 Because as you manoeuvre on a bow line, the bows will swing in towards the pontoon.
4 It is important to keep the bow line under tension to prevent the boat from drifting forward. The only time both engines should be out of gear is momentarily when the line is being released.
5 To check that your radio is working and to set a precedent for security reasons.

8

UNDER WAY

Now that you have successfully left your berth and navigated into open water, we will consider the activities which apply more to open-water boating; for example, if you have a planing boat, how to recognize when it is actually planing and how to trim for maximum speed. We will also discuss what to be aware of when carrying out high-speed manoeuvres, ensuring the safety of your crew as well as other boaters. We will look at how to steer a compass course. During your safety brief, you instructed your crew in their actions, should you have a man overboard situation. In open waters you can practise your man overboard drill with the use of a bucket and fender. Lastly, we will discuss ways of fixing your position, the use of a hand-bearing compass to take a fix and how to plot the fix on a chart.

Planing Speed and Trim

Most planing boats will start to plane in the region of ten to eleven knots. Your

At displacement speed, wash is bubbly and turbulent.

Once planing speed is reached, the wash pattern will change.

wash is the key factor in establishing when planing speed has been reached. Look at your wash as you gradually increase your speed, while making sure that somebody else is keeping a lookout. You will notice that at first the wash is bubbly and turbulent. At around ten knots the wash will start to change. It will form two distinct smooth waves. This change in wash indicates the transition to planing speed.

If you are at sea on a very calm day, once the vessel is planing set the engine revs and start to adjust the trim. Make small adjustments and wait to see the result. When you find the maximum speed, you have the correct trim. Of course, this only applies to calm waters. The trim will need to be altered according to sea state. Trim tabs are often wired in reverse so that the effect is seen on the bow. For example, the port down button will operate the starboard tab and lift the stern, which in turn makes the port bow go down. It is said that 25 per cent of boats have trim tab switches which are incorrectly wired, so check yours.

Trimming for Sea Conditions

Head Sea

Trim the boat bows down so that the deep V forward section of the hull cuts into the waves rather than the flatter aft section slamming into the sea. As the sea state increases, speed may have to be reduced, even to the extent of coming off the plane and working to windward in displacement mode, keeping the seas at an angle to the bow. This results in you tacking the boat backwards and forwards as you would in a yacht.

Following Sea

Trim the boat bows up so that as the boat accelerates down the front of a wave, it does not dig the bows into the trough. Usually higher speeds can be maintained in a following sea and it is possible to keep up planing speeds in quite high sea states.

Athwartships Trim

Trim tabs and power tilt can be used to trim the boat athwartships to counteract any lean caused by wind or ballast. The trim tab nearest the wind is lowered and the leeward one raised to keep the boat running level.

Steering by the Compass

Once the vessel is on the plane and correctly trimmed, you may want to steer a compass course to reach your destination. If your courses are short and you can see the object that you want to reach, possibly a navigation buoy, then instruct your helmsman to head for it and tell him on which side of the boat you want it to pass. However, if you cannot see any reference point, you will want to give your helmsman a 'course to steer'. Remember that you were working in true bearings on the chart, so you need to apply variation and deviation and give a 'compass course to steer' to your helmsman, rounded up or down away from any navigational hazards, as in Fig 41.

Once the course has been achieved, look at the horizon and see if there is any reference point on land which will help. It is quite tiring for the inexperienced helmsman to maintain an accurate

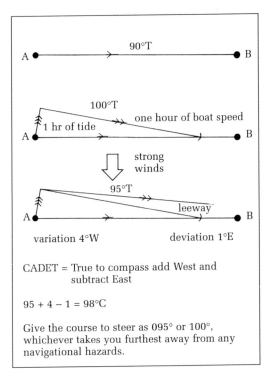

variation 4°W   deviation 1°E

CADET = True to compass add West and
subtract East

95 + 4 − 1 = 98°C

Give the course to steer as 095° or 100°,
whichever takes you furthest away from any
navigational hazards.

Fig 41.

compass course. There is a tendency to become transfixed by the compass and not to look ahead, which is dangerous. If you are navigating in hazardous waters, the more accurate the course that can be steered, the better. Try to give your helmsman a tip to help. For example, if he turns the boat to starboard the numbers will increase on the compass and if he turns the boat to port the numbers will decrease.

High-Speed Manoeuvres

Now that you are at planing speed and cruising in open waters, remember to carry out your engine running checks. Make a note in your log book of oil pressure and water temperature at least every hour. Also check that the batteries are charging and the fuel levels are as expected. Never run your engines at maximum revs for more than a few minutes at a time, reduce by around 200/300 RPM from maximum for cruising. Awareness is very important. Keep a good lookout in all directions at all times, as required under the International Regulations for Preventing Collisions at Sea. If you can see that you are going to cross the wash of another vessel, say 'Stand by wash' to your crew so that they know to hold on. Reduce your speed if necessary. If someone has just gone below to make coffee, let them know if the boat is likely to make any unexpected violent movements. Never let people walk along the side decks and on to the foredeck when under way at speed. You do not want to put your man overboard drill into practice.

Before you carry out any high-speed manoeuvres, take a last look around. Are you going to inconvenience any other vessels, is your wash likely to cause a problem to anyone and are you in sufficient depth of water to carry out your intended manoeuvre? Once you are happy with the situation, warn your crew to hold on before you put the wheel over. Keep one hand on your throttles throughout the manoeuvre to control your speed. If you make your turn too tight, you could suffer the effects of cavitation. Cavitation occurs when the water surrounding the propeller contains an abundance of air bubbles. This air and water mix is less dense than water alone and the propeller is unable to function correctly.

U turns are used to change direction, for instance when you are running outside a main shipping channel and you want to cross over and go back down the other side. You would check behind to make sure the channel was clear, warn your crew, apply wheel to make your turn and straighten up.

Figure of 8 turns could be used to practise applying full helm in one direction, followed by full helm in the opposite direction, a skill required in the man overboard drill. Be aware that you will have to cross your own wash and the boat will swing around a fair amount, so do not forget to tell your crew your intentions and ask them to sit down, before you start your manoeuvres.

The ability to **steer a straight course** is important. If your course is erratic there is less chance of arriving in the right place at the right time. You could also make everyone else onboard feel sick! Look at your wash again – it will indicate if you are steering a straight course. It is more difficult to steer in rough conditions because you may have to steer to the waves.

Emergency stops are not to be carried out without due cause. Warn your crew to hold on, cut the power and carry out a 90 degree turn simultaneously. The larger the boat, the less effect this will have. It is better for the engines to reduce speed slowly if possible and **never** take the controls from full ahead to full astern.

Man Overboard Drill

You are unlikely to have a person fall overboard if you are running a tight ship, warning everyone in times of danger and not allowing your crew to walk along the side decks and on to the foredeck when under way at speed. However, accidents are always possible no matter how careful you are. You should be well practised in your man overboard drill, because if a crew member falls overboard your

reactions need to be automatic. We would also advise you to train your crew in the routine, just in case you happen to be the one who falls in the water.

There is nothing worse for the person in the water than to see you approach and for you to be unable to carry out the rescue. As mentioned in the safety brief, whoever sees the person fall overboard should shout 'Man overboard' to warn everyone onboard that someone is in the water. They should then watch and point. Someone else should grab the nearest lifebelt and throw it in. Following that, he should put on a harness, pick up a boat hook and stand by ready to be told which side the casualty will be picked up. If you are short crewed, or not absolutely sure that you can return to the person in the water and pick them up first time, then also send a Mayday.

You should be well practised in your man overboard drill.

Shout 'Man overboard', watch and point.

The helmsman should immediately alter course by approximately 60 degrees towards the side the person fell in, applying full lock and maintaining speed. Apply opposite wheel and keep the turn going in the opposite direction, until the vessel is running down a reciprocal course.

On the cry of 'Man overboard' the helmsman should immediately alter course by approximately 60 degrees towards the side the person fell in, as illustrated in Fig 42. This action will take the propellers away from the person in the water. Let us imagine that you are steering 000 degrees and your crew member has fallen from the starboard side of your boat. You turn the boat to starboard, applying full lock and maintaining your speed. However, do not wait for the

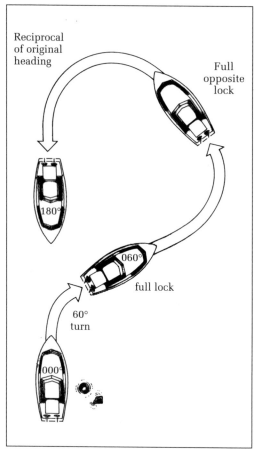

Fig 42(a) Williamson turn

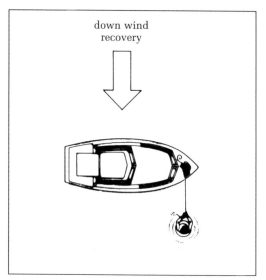

Fig 42(b)

compass to read 060 degrees before you start applying opposite wheel, or you will oversteer. Keep the turn going in the opposite direction, to port, until you are running down a reciprocal course, in this example 180 degrees, eventually running down your own wake. As you see your person in the water reduce speed. At this point, the skipper should take the helm.

There are various ways to approach the man overboard. Whichever way you choose, do it in a slow, controlled manner and keep the person well away from your propellers. Decide which side you will recover the person. Preferably use the side from which you are steering, as this will give you better visibility of the person in the water. Instruct the crew member wearing the harness to clip on and proceed towards the foredeck.

An **upwind approach** has the advantage of pushing you away from the casualty in the water, preventing you from drifting onto him. However, there are many disadvantages to this method of approach. We have already discussed the difficulties of holding a boat 'head to wind', which requires a lot of engine juggling. In addition, the bows could swing across suddenly which is hazardous to the person in the water. The motion of the boat could be quite violent and there is no lee (shelter) for the man in the water. It is difficult to get the speed of approach low, without losing steerage.

The **downwind approach** could therefore be a better option. The disadvantage is that it is possible to drift over the person in the water if your crew cannot

Approach in a slow controlled manner.

Once you have the casualty alongside, cut the engines.

recover him quickly. However, there are many advantages to this method of approach. In appropriate sea states, it is possible to lie beam on to the wind and drift downwind slowly, meaning that there is no need for frantic throttle activity. The boat itself generates a lee for the person in the water. If the motion of the boat is uncomfortable, keep the port or starboard quarter to the wind. In rough conditions, where it would be dangerous to lie beam on, approach with the stern to the wind using the engines astern to control the boat, which can be held against the wind while the person is recovered alongside.

Once you have the person alongside, cut the engines. You now have perhaps the greater problem of getting him back onboard. Recovery strategies should be considered over a cup of coffee alongside,

not in rough conditions with your nearest and dearest on the end of a boat hook. Your bathing platform is a good place to start, even better if you have a bathing ladder which folds down into the water, or you may carry an emergency boarding ladder. Failing that, think about getting him into an inflated dinghy – at least he will be out of the water.

The action you take to recover your man overboard will depend on the construction of your vessel and the ability of the crew which you have onboard at the time. Consider a husband and wife team: the husband weighing 14 stone (dry weight) is the one in the water, and the 9 stone wife has to get him onboard again. If he has been in the water any length of time, he could be suffering from hypothermia and be unable to assist in his own recovery. In this situation she would

Jason's cradle recovery device can be operated by the casualty.

Jason's cradle can be used as a boarding ladder.

probably not be able to do more than secure him alongside. She should have sent out a Mayday as her first priority, to get help as early as possible.

Maintaining a Ship's Log

There are many types of ship's log available. Some have pre-printed columns but we recommend those which are only ruled, allowing you to select headings of your own. We suggest as a minimum:

Passage from	To	Date
Time	Notes	Temp.
Press.	Log	Course
Wind	Baro.	Bilge

Notes in your log should include the engine checks, time you start and stop your engines, time you slip your moorings, any change in course and anything significant which has happened on your passage. If you hear a Mayday, it is very important to write it down. When you are given a berth number on arrival at your destination, write it down or you will have forgotten it by the time you have a fender in your hand. When purchasing fuel, record the amount you put in each tank. Enter any defects which you find, so that you will remember to repair them. If you are steering a straight course for a long time, put an entry in every half an hour along with your estimated position.

By maintaining these records you build a picture which can be useful later. Records in the log can be used to work out fuel consumption, as a reference if you revisit a destination, and it acts as a record of your mileage and qualifying passages if you are working towards Yachtmaster. It can also make good reading and brings back memories years later.

Position Fixing

It can be difficult to orientate yourself at sea, because water looks the same wherever you see it. You therefore need various methods of fixing your position. A position line is a line on which your vessel is known to be. To fix your position on that line, you need to intersect it with another line.

Transits and Leading Lines

A transit is a position line which does not rely on the accuracy of a compass bearing or tidal calculation. It is the alignment of any two conspicuous objects, not neces-sarily put there for that specific purpose, but identifiable on a chart, perhaps a church spire and a chimney. If bearings are specifically for navigation, they are called leading lines and will be marked on the chart. For example, the two sets of lights which lead you into the river Hamble are leading lines. Sometimes there are two posts which line up, perhaps the forward one with a V mark on top and the back one with a ball, which need to be kept in line. Transits and leading lines are often used to navigate safely around the Channel Islands, because tides are strong and it can be difficult to predict them accurately enough to work out courses to steer.

Clearing Bearings

When you are at sea, there will be occasions when navigational hazards exist which are not marked with buoys. You will want to ensure that you do not stray into these dangerous waters. This

The transit into Newtown Creek is a disc in line with a Y shape.

An alternative transit is a mark in the water, in line with an object ashore, such as a house.

can be achieved by the use of a clearing bearing. Draw a line on the chart which keeps you clear of any hazards. Measure the bearing of that line and by keeping your bearing greater than or less than the clearing bearing, as appropriate, you will stay in safe waters.

Depth Contours

Depth contours join areas of equal depth on the sea bed. In areas where the sea bed shelves steeply and has a distinctive pattern, these contours can be used to provide a very accurate method of position fixing. You will need to use your depth sounder, work out the height of tide above chart datum to give actual depth of water and identify the contour line. Such lines could be followed in times of reduced visibility. A line of soundings, shown in Fig 43, can be obtained by making an accurate note of log readings and soundings over a given time. The soundings, reduced to chart datum and with any allowance for tidal set and drift, can then be plotted on to the edge of a

sheet of paper using the scale of the chart in use. The paper's edge is then matched to the chart to find your position. This method only works when the sea bed is distinctive.

Radar Ranges

Radar should be used with due regard to its limitations but can be used in position fixing. The range measuring facility is very accurate, though measuring bearings is not. You could use a radar range along with a compass bearing if visibility permits. Two or preferably three radar ranges will give a very accurate fix (see Fig 44). Measure three ranges using the range rings and draw to scale the corresponding arcs from the positions A, B and C. Only use a radar bearing as a last resort.

Taking a Fix and Plotting it on a Chart

When you are in sight of land, the most common way to find your position is by

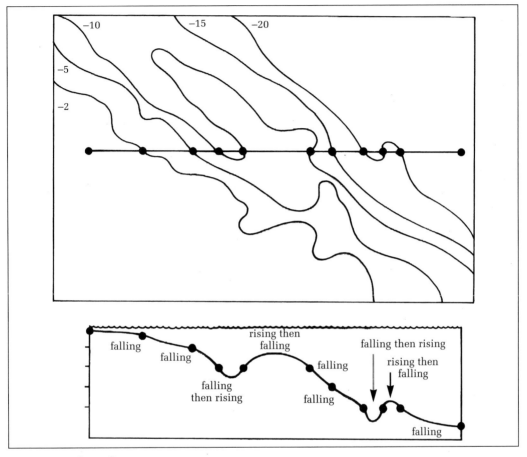

Fig 43   Line of soundings.

taking a fix. To do this you need at least two but preferably three objects which are in sight and identifiable on a navigational chart. You also need a compass, the best type for this job being a hand-bearing compass. They come in various patterns and there will be one to suit you. The conventional prismatic type has a swinging compass card, which can be read while viewing the object concerned. Alternatively, the Fluxgate type gives a digital read-out and the bearings can be stored for later use. Both types have advantages and disadvantages. Personal preference is as important a factor as anything else. It is advisable to go to a chandlery and try them for yourself before you purchase one.

Choose three conspicuous objects on the chart from which to take bearings. The objects should be at least 30 degrees apart, thus giving a good angle of cut. If possible, avoid taking bearings of objects at a great distance because any error will be greater too. If you have to use navigational buoys, remember that they are seldom precisely in their charted position.

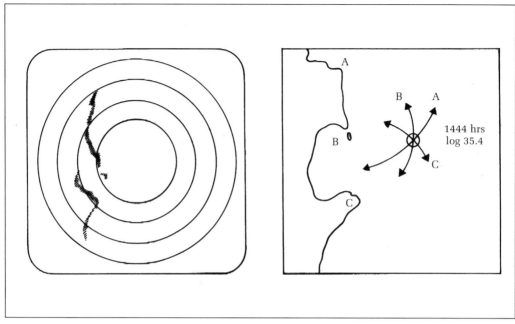

Fig 44   Radar ranges.

Using a hand-bearing compass on deck.

When taking bearings with a hand-bearing compass, go on deck and stand as far away from any metallic object as possible. If you wear metal-rimmed spectacles, check whether they are causing deviation. Take the bearings as quickly as you can and write them down. Take any bearing on the beam last, as this one will have undergone the greatest amount of change if you are underway. Remember to make a note of the log reading and time.

When you have your bearings, go and plot them on your chart. They should be drawn with the arrow pointing from the object out to sea. When you have the fix, you can rub out most of the bearing lines, put a circle around where they cross to represent the fix and write the time and log reading next to it. You will undoubtedly end up with a cocked hat, where the bearings do not come to an exact point. If this is the case, always consider yourself to be in a position nearest to any navigational hazard, as seen in Fig 45. If you have a large cocked hat, check that you have not applied variation in the wrong direction, or identified the object incorrectly.

In Fig 46, the three-bearing fix is taken from a position where the boathouse at the entrance to Beaulieu River bears 027°T. Inchmery House bears 347°T and the Old Coast Guard Cottages bear 286°T. This would give a latitude and longitude of 50° 46′ 20N, 1° 22′ 25W for the entry in your log book, which could be cross checked against a sounding nearby.

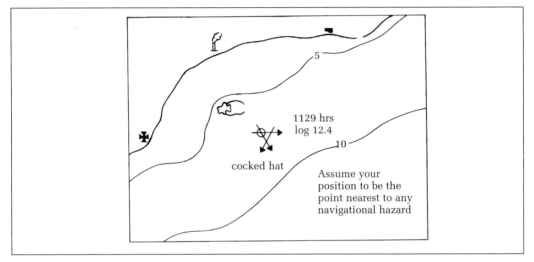

Fig 45   Cocked hat.

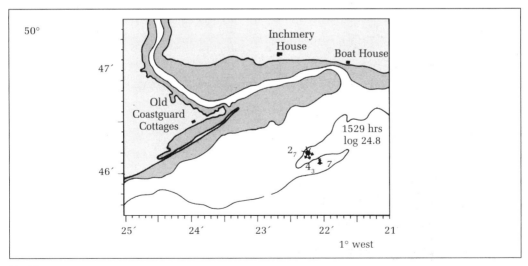

Fig 46.

Summary

When you are underway at speed in open water, always remember to keep a good lookout and pay attention to the safety of your crew. The faster you are travelling, the faster things will happen, so the more vigilance you need. Always maintain a ship's log and enter the time, any notes, engine temperature and oil pressure, log reading, course steered, wind strength and direction, barometric pressure and a note every time you run the bilge. Practise your man overboard drill often, using a downwind approach. Have a strategy for getting people back onboard, remembering that they may not be able to assist in their own recovery and will weigh a lot more when wet. Take time during your journey to practise your position fixing by various methods. Do not just rely on one method which you know works. Try something new and build up your experience.

Questions

1 How will you know when your vessel has reached planing speed?
2 If you were steering a compass course of 180° and your navigator requested a change of course to 200°, which way would you turn the vessel?
3 What precautions would you take when carrying out high-speed manoeuvres?
4 What action should the helmsman take if he hears the shout 'Man overboard'?
5 How many position lines do you need to plot a fix on a chart?

Answers

1 At around ten knots the wash form will start to change. It will no longer be bubbly and turbulent, but will form two distinct smooth waves. This change in wash indicates the transition to planing speed.
2 You would turn the boat to starboard to increase the numbers on the compass.
3 Keep a good lookout, warn everyone to hold on and do not allow your crew to walk along the side decks and on to the foredeck when under way at speed. Keep your hand on the throttles when manoeuvring at speed and always be aware of and give consideration to other vessels.
4 On the cry of 'Man overboard', the helmsman should immediately alter course by approximately 60 degrees towards the side the person fell in, applying full lock and maintaining speed. Apply opposite wheel and keep the turn going in the opposite direction, until the vessel is running down a reciprocal course. As you see your person in the water, reduce speed.
5 Three position lines are most accurate for plotting a fix. They should be separated by 30 degrees if possible.

9

ARRIVING AT YOUR

DESTINATION

In this chapter we will discuss the actions which you should be considering on arrival at your destination. You will need your skipper's notebook again, containing your pilotage notes, which will give any speed limits, local customs and relevant navigational information. We will discuss ways of mooring, with the use of a bow line or spring thrown from onboard. Lastly, we will discuss dinghy stowage, safety precautions and rowing.

Pilotage

Look at your skipper's notebook for information on Cowes, which is your intended destination. Your sketch tells you that there are leading lights into the river at night, but nothing much to help you by day.

Navigation – leading lights 164° bring you safely in. Front light Iso 2s 3m 6M and back light Iso R 2s 5m 3M, visible 120° – 240°.

Green (No3 Fl G 3s) and red (No4 QR) buoys mark the entrance near W shore, yachts must use the main channel and are advised to motor. The speed limit in the harbour is 6 knots.

You may decide to use the bearing of the

leading lights as a leading line to guide you in. Alternatively, you may decide to run in on a bearing from the last buoy, since it is only a short distance. Remember to keep an eye out for any hazards which you have noted. In this example you have:

Hazards – Bramble bank dries to 1.3m to the North. Mud flats and small craft moorings are to the East. Car ferries, hydrofoils and catamarans operate from just inside the entrance.

Since the hydrofoils and catamarans are high-speed craft, remember to keep a good lookout behind. It is easy to become obsessed with navigating and overlook this aspect of safety. You must also give way to any power-driven vessels crossing from your starboard side.

Once you reach the red and green channel markers, you should have reduced your speed to six knots and be monitoring VHF Channel 69.

VHF – All yachts are advised to monitor Ch 69 Cowes Harbour Radio. Marinas use Ch 80. Water taxis listen on Ch 08.

Moorings – visitors' buoys, piles, public pontoon and several marinas.

Some entrances show special lights or marks, details of which will be found in

When you reach the buoys marking the entrance you should have reduced your speed.

almanacs or pilot books. Some marinas will be accessed through a lock. Call the lock keeper on the appropriate VHF channel and ask for instructions. Depending on the state of the tide, you will probably have to wait your turn and go into the lock with several other vessels.

Decide where you are going to moor for the evening. You may wish to use the public pontoons or piles, or you may book a berth in one of the marinas. If you choose a marina you should call the appropriate marina office on their working channel, requesting a berth. Tell the marina master the length of your vessel, how long you wish to stay and if you require shore power. When he responds, he will give you a berth number and advise you which side to hang your fenders. An example of this might be 'Bravo four starboard side to', which assumes that you are going forward into the berth and should rig fenders on the starboard side. Write this down in your log book before you forget it and say it back to him as confirmation. If you are

booking a berth in a marina which is situated on a river, he will also advise you if the berth is on the upstream or downstream side of the trot.

Once you have been advised of a berth, you can ask your crew to rig warps and fenders on the appropriate side. Again, there should be sufficient fenders on the bow and one or two on the opposite side of the boat if there is a vessel in the adjacent berth. Rig stern and bow lines and put a crew member in charge of each. If you only have one crew, rig the stern line and leave it in a safe place while the bow line is attached.

Mooring on to a Pontoon (Shaft Drive)

Find out which way the tide is running by looking at the water. If there is a pile, for example, or another boat which is attached to a pontoon, you will notice the water flowing past it in one direction or the other. Assuming light airs and a

You can see which way the tide is running by looking at a buoy.

Make a controlled approach.

Manoeuvre your vessel so that the crew can throw the bow line ashore and catch a cleat.

Put the outside engine astern to bring the vessel alongside.

choice in your direction of approach, manoeuvre into the tide for maximum control. In strong winds, however, you will need to approach from downwind if possible. If the wind is blowing off the pontoon the momentum of the turn will help to swing the boat towards the pon-toon (Fig 47(d), page 101), counteracting the effect of the wind. If you try to approach from upwind, the wind behind you will almost certainly push the vessel on to the opposite pontoon, or adjacent vessel. If the wind is blowing on to the pontoon, the momentum of the turn will

To help you judge distance, stand at the helm position when alongside and note where the bow appears on the pontoon.

Come down on to the pontoon to see how far away the boat actually is.

Cleats on boat and pontoon in line, the boat will not snatch on the bow line.

help swing the boat away from the pontoon, counteracting the tendency of the wind to push you on to the pontoon before you are fully in the berth. If you try to approach from upwind, the wind behind you will almost certainly push the vessel on to the pontoon far too early.

Manoeuvre your vessel so that the crew on the bow is close enough to throw the bow line ashore and catch a cleat. Unless your crew works in a rodeo, you will need to be quite close to the pontoon in order to give him a fighting chance. Because of the overhanging bows, skippers often think that they are close to hitting a pontoon, when in fact they are still a long way off.

Engaging the outside engine astern with cleats in this position would produce a violent swing toward the pontoon.

The result of this confusion often results in unsavoury language being exchanged between the helm position and the foredeck! To discover the dimensions of your boat, stand at the helm position when your vessel is alongside and look at the bows. Note where the bow appears on the pontoon opposite. Then come down on to the pontoon to see how far away the boat actually is. You could be surprised. The alternative option is to ask your crew to shout the 'distance off' to you, which is sometimes the only method of backing into a berth if you have no view of the stern from your steering position.

Once you have a bow line ashore you have control. By putting your outside engine astern, paddle wheel effect will bring you alongside (Fig 47a). If you are mooring on to a long pontoon, rather than a finger berth, your angle of approach might be steeper. To avoid the boat snatching against the bow line, line up the cleat on the boat with the cleat onshore before you start your swing in toward the pontoon. If you are approaching too fast, put your inside engine astern as well to slow you down. Always keep an engine in gear if possible, to avoid the bow rope slacking.

If the wind is fresh and blowing you away from the pontoon, it is important to get the bow line ashore quickly as the boat will not stay alongside for long. Once the bow rope is secure, if the outer engine running astern is not powerful enough to pull your stern in against the wind, help it by turning the wheel away from the pontoon and using the inside engine ahead at fewer revs (Fig 47b).

If the wind is blowing you on to a long pontoon, position your vessel parallel to the pontoon and allow the wind to blow you alongside, maintaining the parallel attitude with small amounts of power as appropriate.

When manoeuvring on a spring, the warp needs to be much longer than a bow line.

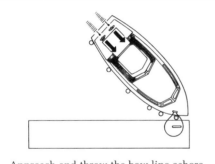

Approach and throw the bow line ashore.

Turn the helm away from the pontoon and put the inside engine ahead to bring the boat alongside. Occasional use of the outside engine astern will keep the boat parallel to the pontoon.

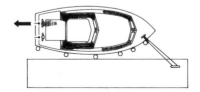

Helm to midships. Outside engine astern.

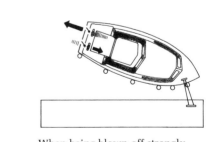

When being blown off strongly, outside engine astern, helm away from pontoon, inside engine ahead at fewer revs.

Fig 47(a)   **Shaft drive.**

Fig 47(b).

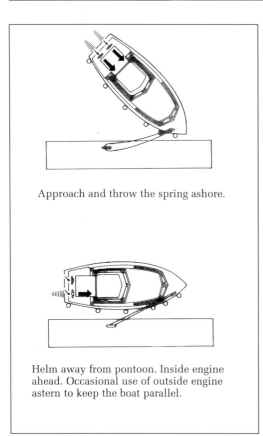

Approach and throw the spring ashore.

Helm away from pontoon. Inside engine ahead. Occasional use of outside engine astern to keep the boat parallel.

Fig 47(c)   **Shaft drive using a spring.**

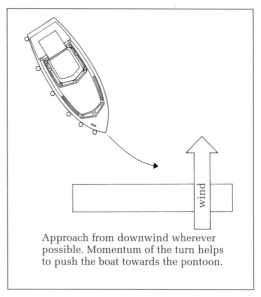

Approach from downwind wherever possible. Momentum of the turn helps to push the boat towards the pontoon.

Fig 47(d).

Mooring on to a Pontoon (Outdrive)

Rig warps and fenders the same as for shaft drive boats. Once the bow line is secure, in light airs the outdrive vessel will usually come alongside by turning the wheel towards the pontoon and engaging the outside engine astern. If the conditions are fresh and you are being blown away from the pontoon, put both engines astern to give a greater effect and bring the vessel alongside.

If conditions are very brisk, you may need to consider the use of a spring. Once the spring is ashore and secured, turn your wheel away from the pontoon and engage your inside engine ahead to bring the vessel alongside (see Fig 48).

Using a Spring

Heavy displacement boats will respond more successfully with the use of a spring, a technique which might be considered by a lighter vessel in brisk conditions. Throw the spring ashore, turn the helm away from the pontoon and put the inside engine ahead to bring the vessel alongside. Keep the boat parallel to the pontoon by occasional use of the outside engine astern (see Fig 47(c)).

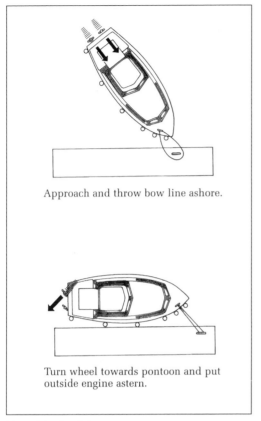

Approach and throw bow line ashore.

Turn wheel towards pontoon and put outside engine astern.

Fig 48(a) **Outdrive.**

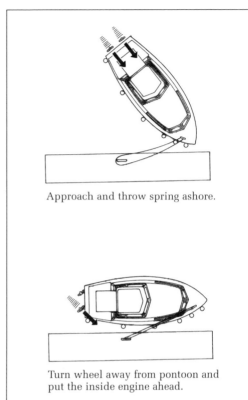

Approach and throw spring ashore.

Turn wheel away from pontoon and put the inside engine ahead.

Fig 48(b) **Outdrive using a spring.**

Once alongside, you will be asked to pay!

Mooring Alongside Another Vessel

If you are mooring in a river it is common to have to raft, which entails mooring against another vessel. It is courteous to ask the other skipper before you attach yourself to his vessel. Try to pick a vessel of comparable size to your own. Rig your fenders high so that the widest part of the hulls are protected from each other. The people on the other boat may offer to take your lines for you. If they do not, spend as short a time as possible onboard and never walk through their cockpit, try to go

When moored alongside another vessel, always attach shore lines.

around the foredeck. Attach your lines to their cleats and bring the warps back onboard your own vessel. Never leave piles of your rope onboard other boats.

Next, you should attach shore lines, so that the first boat in the raft is not taking the weight of every other boat on its lines. This also allows any boat to be removed from the raft at any time without involving every other vessel. You may be able to walk your lines ashore, or you may have to launch your dinghy. The common way of attaching to a communal cleat or bollard is to pass your bowline through the eye of every other bowline on the bollard. Again, this enables any boat to leave at any time without removing every other vessel's lines.

Dinghy Practice and Safety

Many motor boats carry a dinghy permanently inflated on davits. This method of stowage makes launching quick and easy. If you carry a deflated dinghy, you will need to pump it up before use. It is easier to do this and launch it from a pontoon than from your boat. It can be fun to visit less popular harbours and anchorages where you will need a dinghy to get ashore. Always take the pump with you and wear a life-jacket when you are in a dinghy, especially on your way back from the pub! If you are out at night, it is prudent to carry a torch as a warning signal to other craft.

Rowing is an art in itself and should be practised. If the tide or wind is strong it can be difficult to row even a short distance. Some tenders have small engines, but if the engine fails, you still have to row, so remember to take your oars. It is usual to row with your back to the bow and pull the boat through the water. However, we know many women who are inefficient at rowing this way round, but are quite proficient if they row the other way, in effect pushing the boat through the water. This anomaly is possibly related to upper arm strength.

Taking on Fuel

At some point you will need to take on fuel. There is information in the almanac as we have seen, advising if fuel is available at your port of call. When you approach a fuel berth, be aware that there might be a lot of traffic manoeuvring on and off the pontoons, with waiting vessels milling around. Make your approach in exactly the same way that you would for any other pontoon. There will often be someone there to take your lines for you. When you are alongside, switch off your engines and do not allow anyone onboard to smoke. Diesel has a higher flash point than petrol and does not give off inflammable vapour, but care should still be taken.

You will probably have two fuel tanks. It is advisable to keep the cross-connector closed at all times and to fill each tank independently. This way you remove the risk of cross-contamination from one tank to another by keeping them isolated. If you leave the cross-connector open, it is

also possible for fuel to pass from one tank to the other when under way. For example, if you have a slight list to starboard when you start, after a while you could have a large list and the majority of your fuel in your starboard tank.

Have a bucket of hot soapy water ready and quickly wipe around the fuel filler cap before you remove it. This will help prevent diesel stains. As the tank becomes full, you will hear noises coming from the breather. At this point, put soapy water around the breather itself and the hull beneath it. When fuel drips out you know the tank is full and you can wash away any excess. Replace the filler cap, make a note of the amount of fuel and repeat the exercise for the other tank. You might like to lift the hose as it is carried across your deck, as dragging can sometimes leave black marks.

Note in your log book the fuel which has been put into each tank and make your departure. If you ask the attendant, he will usually write this information on your receipt for you to save you wasting time on his pontoon when he is busy.

Have a bucket of soapy water ready to wipe away diesel spills.

Lift the hose to avoid marking your decks.

Summary

Time spent planning ahead is always worth while. If you have detailed pilotage notes in your skipper's notebook, it will take the pressure off as you approach a new harbour. You will have a good idea of what to expect and remember that you will have collision regulations to think about as well as pilotage. Rig your fenders so that you have the usual protection on the bows near the waterline for pontoons and on the other side of your vessel if there are craft nearby. Fenders will need to be higher if you are mooring alongside another vessel. Manoeuvre your vessel on a bow line for planing boats or a spring if you have a heavy displacement boat. Once you have a bow line ashore you are in control. Encourage your crew to communicate with you so that you know when there is a line ashore for you to manoeuvre against. Always be aware of safety when taking on fuel and using a dinghy.

Questions

1 What does the following mean in a pilot book, with reference to leading lights: Front light Iso 2s 3m 6M and back light Iso R 2s 5m 3M, visible 120° – 240°?
2 If the wind is strong and the predominant element, is the preferred method of approaching a pontoon mooring from upwind or downwind?
3 If you were rafting against other boats for a short lunchtime visit to a pub, would you need to put lines ashore?
4 What safety precautions should you observe when you are making a trip in a dinghy?
5 If you have two fuel tanks, should you keep the cross-connector open or closed?

Answers

1 The front light is white, three metres high, isophase every two seconds and visible for six miles. The back light is red, five metres high, isophase every two seconds and visible for three miles. Both are visible when approaching from a bearing between 120° and 240°. An isophase light has equal periods of light and dark.
2 In strong winds, a downwind approach is preferred. This way the swing of the boat is into the wind and towards the pontoon. If you try to approach from upwind, the wind behind you will almost certainly push the vessel on to the adjacent boat or pontoon.
3 Yes, it is very unseamanlike not to. Shore lines prevent the first boat in the raft from taking the weight of every other boat on its lines. They also allow any boat to be removed from the raft at any time and since the others were there before you, it is feasible that they will want to leave first.
4 Always wear a life-jacket when in a dinghy. Make sure you are a competent rower and capable of making your passage. Take the pump with you and carry a warning torch at night. If you have an engine on your dinghy, take your oars as a back-up.
5 Keep the cross-connector closed. This stops fuel contamination between tanks and also prevents fuel moving from one tank to the other when under way.

10

ADVANCED MOORING
TECHNIQUES

Once you have mastered pontoon moorings, your boating can become a little more adventurous. Quiet anchorages are preferred by some cruisers and visitors' buoys can also be tranquil. There is the advantage that people cannot walk past your boat and disturb you and you might also be privileged enough to witness some spectacular wildlife. Although piles may be your mooring of choice, in popular months you will undoubtedly end up in a raft. All of these techniques will be discussed in this chapter. We will also cover night cruising and one technique to really impress your neighbours, that of ferry gliding.

Anchoring

There are many different patterns of anchor, each with its own individual advantages and disadvantages. It is said that the Bruce anchor was developed by someone trying to plough the sea bed looking for buried cable. It always got stuck! Whichever pattern you choose, make sure it is heavy enough to hold your vessel. All anchors work by being pulled in a horizontal direction. In order to achieve this, you need plenty of anchor warp or chain on the sea bed. The majority of motor boats will have only chain attached to the anchor. If you use

Visitors' buoys can be tranquil, especially out of season.

An Admiralty Stockless anchor in hawsepipe stowage.

A Delta anchor stowed on a bow roller.

Rig an anchor ball to let other vessels know you are at anchor.

this method, then you will need at least four times the maximum expected depth in calm conditions. More will be required if it is windy or the tide is really strong. If you use a mixture of chain and warp, then you will need six times the maximum expected depth and even up to ten times in bad conditions. Nylon is the best warp as it will sink and also stretch up to thirty per cent, helping to absorb shock, before it breaks.

The first thing to do is to look at your chart and decide where you want to anchor. There are then several points to consider, even if the anchorage is empty. Check the quality of the bottom; firm sand or thick mud are best. Work out the minimum expected depth for the duration of your stay to ensure that you do not ground. Also calculate the maximum expected depth and ensure that you have enough chain to hold your anchor on the bottom. Identify suitable bearings or transits to check that the anchor is not dragging. Look at the proximity of other vessels. You must be clear to swing with

the tide and ensure that you do not foul other anchor chains. Do not pick a lee shore in a strong wind, or if the wind is forecast to increase. If you are planning a trip ashore, look for a suitable landing place. For those who feel seasick at anchor, pick an anchorage away from a busy waterway to cut down on wash from other craft.

Once you are organized, rig the tripping line if you have one and motor in towards your chosen spot. Head into wind or tide, whichever is stronger. Stop the boat and lower the anchor to the bottom in a controlled manner. The crew can then pay out the calculated amount of chain, again in a controlled manner, as the boat is slowly driven backward. It is useless to drop twenty metres of chain over the side so that it lands in a heap. Look for evidence of dragging, by seeing if the chain is jumping. Double-check by taking bearings. Rig an anchor ball in the forward part of the vessel, in accordance with the collision regulations, to let others know that you are at anchor.

Picking Up a Mooring Buoy

Before picking up a mooring buoy, take a good look around. You will seldom find a single buoy, so look at the others and see how the boats are lying to them. This should give you an indication as to the best direction of approach. Try that direction first, but if it does not feel right, don't be afraid to take a different line.

The standard approach for picking up a mooring buoy is into tide, providing as always that the wind is not too strong. We have mentioned several times that it is difficult to hold a motor boat 'head to wind'. If the wind is the stronger element, a stern to wind approach could be considered. Running the engines astern will hold the boat against the wind until the bow line is secure. The boat will naturally turn head on to the wind once secure.

1. Some mooring buoys have a marker buoy attached.

2. Pick up the marker buoy with a boat hook.

3. This line is attached to a heavy rope, which is usually muddy.

4. Add a securing line for safety.

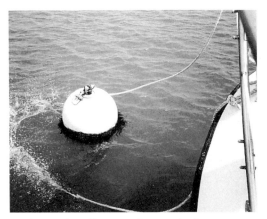

1. Throw a bow line over the mooring buoy.

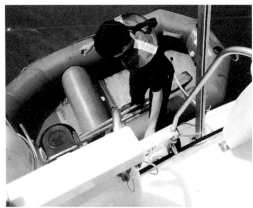

2. Launch your dinghy.

3. Attach a bow rope to the eye of the buoy with a turn.

4. This bow line can be secured with a long bowline which may be released from onboard.

There are various ways of attaching your vessel to the mooring buoy, but those which involve the crew working from the bow are preferred. There is a school of thought that suggests the crew should work from the bathing platform. We discourage this method for two reasons. Firstly, if the crew falls in he will be very near to the propellers and, secondly, ropes can foul propellers.

Some buoys have a line already attached with a marker buoy on the end. If your crew can pick this up with a boat hook, it is the easiest method. The line holding the marker buoy is attached to the heavy rope of the mooring buoy. It is also advisable to attach a securing line of your own. The rope is usually muddy so do not carry out this procedure in your best white trousers!

If there is no marker buoy, then throw a bow line over the mooring buoy, in the same manner used for cleats on pontoons. Use any rope except polyprop, as you

Once all the hard work is done, you can enjoy lunch!

want the rope to sink beneath the buoy. This will hold you until you can attach a bow rope to the eye on the top of the buoy. You may be able to reach from the bows of your vessel to do this, or on larger vessels you may have to launch the dinghy. Do not leave the boat with a line thrown over the buoy for long, as it is not secure and the rope will chafe.

Mooring Between Piles

When mooring between piles you will need two long lengths of rope, one for the bow and another for the stern. Put a bowline in one end of each rope and coil them neatly on deck to ensure free running.

Again, look around at other nearby vessels. If there are boats attached to mooring buoys or at anchor, look at the direction in which they are lying and it will give you an indication of the best direction of approach. Fender the bow at

its widest point, which could even be the guard-rail stanchions themselves. Drive the boat up to the front pile; try not to touch it, but get very close so that your crew can thread the bow line through the ring on the pile. Bring the rope back under the guard-rails and secure to the cleat using the bowline. The line is now controlled using the free end coiled on deck.

Once secure, back away a few metres and judge how the boat is going to behave. You need the vessel to be on the leeward side of the stern pile to maintain control. Your crew on the bow can let rope out, controlling it on the cleat as you back towards the pile on the stern. Your crew in charge of the stern line should advise you when he is opposite the pile. Again, make sure a fender is attached to protect the boat. You can now manoeuvre on the bow rope and swing in towards the stern pile, by engaging the outside engine astern. If you are going too quickly, put the other engine astern as well to slow you down. It is better to keep an engine in gear at all times and keep tension on the bow line to maintain control. If conditions are really fresh, you may need to apply wheel to help the swing. Your crew can then lean over the side and thread a warp through the ring on the stern pile.

Once the stern line is attached, you can move forward taking in the bow line and letting out the stern line, until you are somewhere in the middle of the two piles. These slip lines are not suitable to hold the vessel for any length of time and should be supplemented by mooring lines, tied to the rings with the use of your dinghy.

If there is already a vessel between the piles and you have to make a raft, then

Secure lines to the rings with the use of a dinghy.

The completed pile mooring.

moor alongside the vessel in the normal way, using a bow line, stern line and springs. You should moor against the leeward side of the vessel so that you are not being pushed against its lines by the wind. Once secure against the vessel, attach lines to the piles with the use of your dinghy.

Night Cruising

Although the Day Skipper is intended to be out in daylight, the practical course does include some night hours just in case you are inadvertently out in the dark. If you are not attending a course, pick an area which you know well, or take a more experienced person with you on your first outing at night. You should experience night cruising on a bright moonlit night, with light airs, not in the teeth of a gale.

Things change quite dramatically at night. Familiar landmarks which give you information regarding your position by day are gone from sight. Background shore lights can confuse the picture, often making navigation lights difficult to identify. Other vessels are no longer easily identifiable by shape, you only have their small navigation lights to help you. Floating hazards are no longer visible, so consequently you should always reduce your speed. Always wear life-jackets and preferably helm from outside to give you better vision.

If you have to use a searchlight for any reason, take care not to shine it at other boats because you will destroy their night vision for a few minutes. For the same reason it is advisable for one person on your boat to close their eyes or look away while the light is on.

It is very difficult to judge distance at night. The size of the light on a navigational mark is very small, and there is therefore very little alteration in the size as you approach. There is also virtually no contrast at night and it is difficult to judge the distance between an object and its background. Because of these difficulties in perception, it is a common anomaly that when you perceive the light to be near, you are actually in imminent danger of hitting the buoy.

Ferry Gliding

If you find yourself in a situation where there is a very strong tide running but very little wind, it is an ideal time to

Hold the vessel stationary against the tide, opposite your berth. Turn the wheel towards the pontoon, putting the tide on the outside bow.

practise the art of ferry gliding. If you perfect this skill you can have the benefit of squeezing into a tight mooring which nobody else felt they could negotiate! Manoeuvre your vessel, bows into the tide, opposite a pontoon with an available mooring. Pick a long pontoon until you are more experienced. First adjust the engine controls so that you are holding the vessel stationary against the tide. While you practice this technique your crew could occupy themselves rigging warps and fenders. Keep watching the pontoon; the objective is to keep the vessel stationary relative to the mooring you intend to take.

When you have mastered this, either turn the wheel towards the pontoon, or alter the engine controls to put the tide on your outside bow. By keeping the boat in this position, the tide will glide your vessel sideways on to the pontoon. To get off again, rig a back spring, gently edge the bow out, being careful not to damage your bathing platform, and let the tide work on the inside bow to take you off the pontoon.

Keep the vessel stationary relative to the mooring.

The tide will glide your vessel sideways on to the pontoon.

The art is in keeping the boat stationary relative to the pontoon and changing the tide from one bow to the other to achieve sideways movement.

Summary

Anchoring, picking up mooring buoys and mooring between piles are all alternatives to marina berths. You may have privacy and tranquillity, but you will not have shore power, shops or other facilities. However, in more remote harbours, these moorings may be your only option, so you should practise these mooring techniques. Night cruising is something everyone should experience during optimum visibility and calm sea state, unless you have an experienced person onboard. Always wear life-jackets and keep your speed down when out in the dark. Once you are confident with your boat handling, try your hand at ferry gliding, which really is useful in conditions of strong tide and light winds.

Questions

1   How many times the maximum expected depth of chain will you need to anchor? What is the ratio if you use warp?
2   What are the considerations to be taken when anchoring?
3   When mooring between piles, which line would you attach first?
4   What are the conditions of wind and tide for successful ferry gliding?

Answers

1   If you use chain only, you will need at least four times the maximum expected depth in calm conditions. More will be required if it is windy or the tide is really strong. If you use a mixture of chain and warp, you will need six times the maximum expected depth and even up to ten times in bad conditions.
2   Check that the bottom is suitable to hold you; firm sand or thick mud are best. Work out the minimum expected depth for the duration of your stay to ensure that you do not ground. Work out the maximum expected depth and ensure that you have enough anchor cable to hold your anchor on the bottom. Identify suitable bearings or transits to check that the anchor is not dragging. Look at the proximity of other vessels; you must be clear to swing with the tide and ensure that you do not foul their anchor chains. Do not pick a lee shore in a strong wind, or if the wind is forecast to increase. If you are planning a trip ashore you will need a suitable landing place.
3   Always attach the bow line first, because with a bow line attached you have control of a twin-screw motor boat.
4   Light winds and strong tides are required for ferry gliding.

11

EMERGENCIES

This is the chapter which we hope you will never need. We will discuss engine failure, single-engine handling, towing, accepting a tow, fire and sinking. Many safety aspects have already been covered in Chapter 2. Heavy-weather handling and cruising in restricted visibility will also be considered. It is foolish to think that you can ignore the possibility of having to deal with adverse weather, because although you might embark in fine weather, conditions can deteriorate very quickly. It is always better to be forearmed.

Engine Failure

To ensure that you get the best out of your boat it is vitally important to conduct at least a minimum amount of preventative maintenance. This will minimize unnecessary breakdowns at sea and reduce the chances of expensive repair work being required. It is also important from the aspect of good seamanship. The skipper of any vessel is wholly responsible for the safety and well-being of his or her ship and crew. Time and again, cruises are spoilt due to lack of preparation or the inability to rectify minor faults and problems.

Petrol engines are lighter in weight and less expensive than diesel engines. However, the associated electrics in the marine environment, higher fuel costs and flammability of petrol do not make them a first choice for pleasure boats. The rule with any engine, be it petrol or diesel, is to keep it clean and properly maintained. Engine failure can occur for various reasons, the more common being lack of fuel; dirt, air or water in the fuel; clogged air filters or overheating problems.

Diesel fuel is taken from the tank and then passed through the primary filter. Often this filter has a water trap which can be checked by eye. If not, you may need to drain a little fuel into a container in order to check it for water or debris, by means of the drain on the bottom of the filter. This filter should be checked once a month and more often if water is found. The fuel lift pump lifts fuel from the tank towards the engine. There is usually a manual lever on the lift pump which can be used to bleed the system. The engine fine filter is next, followed by the injection pump. It is imperative that water does not find its way to the injection pump and injectors as resultant damage will be very costly.

You will need to bleed the system after

Drain or change the primary filter using a bucket.

Engine temperature gauges should be checked as you increase the revs of your engines. It is not uncommon to pick up a plastic bag over the water intake, or a substantial amount of weed in the strainers, particularly when manoeuvring at slow speeds. When speed is increased, the engine subsequently overheats. Most motor boats will have a sea-water and fresh-water cooling system. The sea-water system can fail if the sea cocks are closed, the strainers are clogged, there is a blockage in the system or the impeller fails. The fresh-water system coolant levels may be low, V belts may be slack or broken, there may be a leak in the system or the thermostat can fail.

It is possible that you may have to close down an engine when there is actually nothing wrong with it, for instance if you pick up a rope around the propeller. If you have outdrives, you can stop both engines, remove the ignition keys for safety, raise the leg and remove the rope. You have more of a problem with a shaft drive vessel. If the rope is attached to an object or you can see the end of it, try to hold it with a boat hook and run the engine slowly astern. If cutters are fitted

any maintenance, such as a filter change, or if air has been drawn into the system for any other reason, such as running out of fuel. Starter motors should not be run for more than fifteen seconds at a time, with a three- or four-minute break between operations. Therefore, do not bleed your engine on the starter. Slacken the screw on the engine filter and operate the lift pump manually until fuel appears. Tighten the screw and slacken the pipe union to one of the injectors. Put a rag over the injector to protect your eyes and skin. Diesel at this pressure is capable of being injected through the skin. Run the engine for a maximum of ten seconds on the starter. Fuel should have appeared on the rag; if it has, tighten the union. Do the same with a second injector and the engine will probably start. It is better to ask someone else to operate the starter if possible.

Rope cutter fitted to a shaft.

they should cut the rope, but some may remain on the shaft leading to imbalance. If you have no cutters, you will have to call for assistance, or put someone in the water to cut the rope. They should preferably wear a dry or wet suit and mask. Again, stop both engines, remove the ignition keys if fitted and securely attach the person to the boat by a rope. Beware of the dangers of cold water. If the rope is not attached to an object, you can simply progress slowly on one engine.

Single-Engine Handling

Most of the increased reliability of a twin-engined vessel over a single-engined vessel comes from having two independent propulsion systems. If one engine fails, it should be possible to return the boat to a safe situation using the other. Practise handling the boat using just one engine. The principles are the same as those which would be used when handling a single-engined vessel, the most important consideration being the paddle wheel effect (PWE). It is important to know which way your propellers rotate as this will determine the turning capabilities of the boat. Call the marina, by VHF, requesting an easy berth if your normal berth is confined.

With only the port engine available, the boat will turn easily to starboard since PWE, turning moment (TM) and slip-stream effect all favour the turn. However, when turning to port PWE and TM still try to turn the boat to starboard. The only effect trying to turn the boat to port is the slip-stream effect which, because of the small size of the rudders on a fast boat, is poor at slow speed. Initially the boat will turn to starboard until there is sufficient

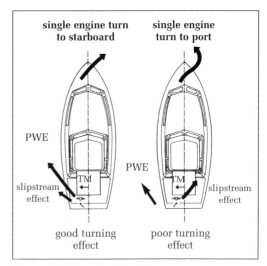

Fig 49   Single-engine handling.

water flow for the slip-stream effect on the rudders to overcome the starboard turning effects of the PWE and TM (see Fig 49). In a purpose-built single-engined boat, TM would not exist since the propeller would be on the centre line. Furthermore, slip-stream effect would be greater due to a larger rudder.

Bringing the Boat Alongside – Port Engine Only

The rule of thumb is as follows: rig fenders on the side of the failed engine and find a berth where you can approach into wind and/or tide in the normal preferred fashion. As you approach the pontoon, keep in mind that it is easy to turn the boat towards the pontoon, but she will be slow to react if you wish to turn away from the pontoon. Avoid approaching at too steep an angle. Having secured the bow line, going astern on the available engine will paddle wheel the boat towards the pontoon and hold it alongside as in normal berthing.

Turning in a Confined Space with a Single Engine

We have seen that, when turning the twin screw boat on one engine only, the turn in the direction of the failed engine produces the tightest turn, i.e. turn to starboard for starboard engine failure. However, this will at best produce a turning circle of about two and a half to three boat lengths.

Should you be in a confined situation, where you need to turn completely round and where the available width is, say, one and a half boat lengths, then you have a problem. Backing out is not an option. The boat will be impossible to steer astern

since PWE will always be stronger than slip stream effect. The technique you will adopt will be familiar to single-engine boaters already, to turn in what is apparently the wrong direction, i.e. for a starboard engine failure, turn to port. Follow the sequence in Fig 50.

Put the helm fully to port and leave it there. Start by giving a reasonable burst ahead on the port engine. A reasonable burst for most boats is probably up to about 1,000 engine rpm. Initially the boat will tend to turn to starboard due to the PWE and TM effects, but as the slipstream effect becomes more pronounced, you should detect the boat starting to swing to port. At this stage, you will

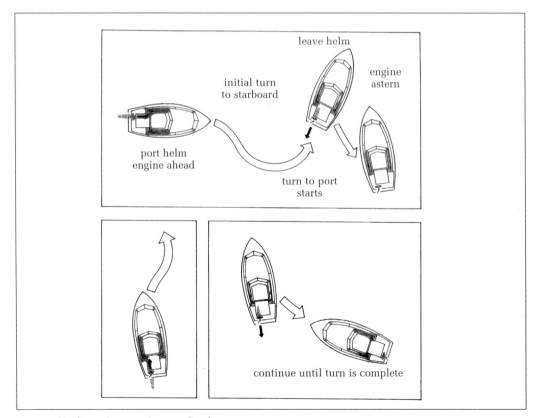

Fig 50   **Single engine turn in a confined space.**

probably start to run out of room ahead. Now go astern on the port engine up to 1,000 rpm (leave the wheel alone!) and use the PWE to swing the stern to starboard. Pull back as far as you dare before going ahead on the port engine and repeating the previous step. With most twin screw boats, most of the turn occurs when going astern. Some boats may show no tendency at all to turn to port when going ahead and all the turning effect must come from the astern movements. Continue in this manner until you have completed the turn.

Towing and Accepting a Tow

If you become involved in towing, you will need to ensure that the towing vessel has enough power to pull the tow. You will also need a suitable length of line and a securing point on which to attach the tow line. One major problem is chafe, so go through a fairlead if you have one. In a following sea, the towed vessel tends to surge into the stern of the towing vessel. The towed vessel should tow something itself to prevent this happening, such as a drogue or length of warp.

The line must be strong and should be as long as possible. Nylon is best. Some consider the anchor and chain to be a sensible option, attaching the tow line to the anchor of the towed vessel and paying out the chain a suitable distance. The weight of the anchor acts as a damper to reduce snatching of the line.

It is difficult to pass a line into the wind, but it is safer to approach from the lee side. Tying a line to a fender and drifting it downwind from a distance, to the vessel requiring a tow, is often a sensible procedure in really rough conditions.

Towing astern affects manoeuvrability, whereas towing alongside will be a better option in calm conditions, such as when you reach harbour and need to put the tow alongside. The bow spring of the towing vessel will be the line which takes the strain with this arrangement.

Anyone giving you a tow can be in a position to claim salvage. Make your position clear and pass them your lines if possible. Try to ensure any agreements are witnessed.

Fire

Fire can kill in minutes, smoke can kill in seconds, so always have your escape route clear before fighting a fire. Prevention is better than cure and procedures for gas management were discussed in Chapter 2. Check that your fuel pipes do not run close to the exhaust pipes. Check your sea-water strainers regularly, because if the inlet is blocked the exhausts will not be cooled and they could melt and catch fire. Fumes are heavier than air so run engine-room fans and bilge pumps as appropriate. Turn the power off to any appliance which is not required when leaving the vessel, but leave the automatic bilge pumps on. Use the correct fuses for electrical equipment, only allow smoking on deck, do not deep fry onboard or leave pots unattended in the galley when under way. Fuel + Heat + Oxygen = Fire. To put a fire out, you need to remove one of these elements. Fire blankets should be left over the fire for at least thirty minutes to ensure that it does not reignite. Halon is useful for getting into inaccessible corners but is toxic and more often used in engine-rooms. Dry powder should be pointed at the base of the fire. Take care not to spread a fuel fire with the jet from a fire extinguisher. Burning plastics can give off very poisonous fumes and plastic hatches can distort and jam in a fire. If the fire is on the stern, turn the vessel head to wind if possible, so that the fire is blown away from the rest of the boat and vice versa.

Sinking

If water is entering the boat it is usually from a sea cock or from the engine, unless of course you have hit something and made a hole in the hull. Try to identify where the water is coming in. If it is from a sea cock, close it. If it is from the engine, stop it. If it is a hole, then put a soft wooden bung into it, or put a cushion in a plastic bag over the hole and stand on it. Bilge pumps may not be powerful enough to keep the water under control. Once the batteries are submerged you will not have power, so make your distress or urgency call as soon as it becomes obvious that you are not in control. Engine-mounted bilge pumps are a bonus in such conditions as they can remove a lot of water and if diesel powered will continue to run without electrical power. Hand pumps are exhausting to operate for more than a short while. You could close the inlet sea cock to the heads, disconnect the hose and use the toilet as a pump.

As already mentioned, if you are near the coast, you might consider beaching the boat in the interest of saving your crew. However, if you cannot keep the water at bay and are offshore, you will have little option but to abandon ship. Make sure all your crew are in warm clothes and wearing life-jackets. Launch the life-raft (details in Chapter 2) and also take the dinghy. Rafts are most likely to capsize during boarding in rough conditions and high winds. Sit upwind to help prevent this. The drogue is important as it gives the raft stability. Ensure that it is streamed on a long line, allowing it to sink below the wave action. Close the hatch and maintain the raft.

If you do not have a life-raft, you will be in the water in a life-jacket. Cold water shock will last about three minutes, in which time you will experience rapid breathing and shivering. Once this subsides, cross your hands over your life-jacket, cross your ankles and curl up to conserve warmth. If there are several of you, try to stay together, either in a line or a circle. If conditions are rough, link your fingers together, seal around your nose with your thumbs and breath behind your hands to stop yourself breathing in sea spray.

Fog/Blind Pilotage

At sea, especially in fog, accurate perception of direction and distance of, for example, a fog horn is difficult. Fog consists of air saturated with water droplets and actually carries sound far better than dry air. Very soft sounds can be carried a long way in fog. However, without sight of the source of sound, you are not able to detect whether it is a loud sound travelling a long distance, or a soft sound travelling a short distance. High frequency is filtered out over distance, so distant noises sound dull. Thunder is a perfect example.

As soon as you see fog approaching, take a fix and note the depth. It is a known fact that people tend to travel round in circles when they are cut off from sensory input, so you must have an accurate initial position and then trust your instruments. You should adjust your speed accordingly, hoist your radar reflector if it is not a permanent fixture, switch on your navigation lights and keep a good lookout and listening watch. Your crew should be in life-jackets and warm clothing. If you are in a busy shipping area try to manoeuvre into shallow water and perhaps anchor. You should have white flares to hand, sound the appropriate fog signal and monitor your radar if you have one. If you are out at sea and heading for a harbour, aim off to one side of it so that you know which way to turn as you approach the coast. When deciding which side to approach, consider wind, tide, navigational hazards, etc. The main danger when cruising in fog is being run down.

Heavy-Weather Handling

As we have already said, the definition of heavy weather will vary from one boat to another. However, if the conditions of the wind and sea start to dictate the handling and course of the vessel, then you are in heavy weather. By monitoring the weather (see Chapter 5), these situations can be predicted and avoided. There are comparatively few harbours which can be entered safely in rough conditions and in any state of tide. We are lucky in the Solent in that most marinas are tucked away in rivers and the Isle of Wight provides much protection against really bad sea conditions. This is one reason why the Solent makes such a good training ground.

If you have to remain at sea, give

yourself plenty of room. Stay away from shipping lanes, tidal races and shallow water. Make sure that all crew members are wearing life-jackets and harnesses if you think there is any risk of losing someone overboard. Stow all gear above and below decks. Ensure that all fixtures on deck are secure, for instance the dinghy or life-raft, and check that all hatches and locker lids are battened down. Take a fix before the visibility is reduced and go to the loo, one of the most difficult manoeuvres in rough conditions!

If the sea is really rough, consider tacking the boat as you would a sailing boat, so that the wind is on the port or starboard bow and the passage of the boat is at an angle to the waves, rather than head on into them.

Although not emergencies, the following two paragraphs discuss common inconveniences.

Seasickness

Medication to prevent seasickness needs to be taken in advance and often produces drowsiness. Medication has little effect once sickness starts. The only guaranteed cure for seasickness is to sit under a tree!

Seasickness is caused by perceptual confusion between your eyes and your organs of balance. Therefore, you are less likely to feel sick outside helming, where you can see the horizon and approaching wave pattern. Standing and compensating for the movement of the boat is preferable to sitting and being passively moved around.

Adaptation to the motion will eventually occur, usually after a day or two. A bout of seasickness often gives immunity for six to ten weeks, but is specific to the one vessel. This is why skippers and crew are often sick on the first passage of the year but not for the rest of the season. Remember, if you have never been seasick, you have probably not found the right situation or motion to trigger you.

Car Journey Home

Having enjoyed your time afloat, take care during the car journey home. Many people still feel the movement of the boat for a few hours after they set foot on dry land. You will probably have spent your time afloat travelling at less than thirty knots. For a while everything will appear to be happening very fast on the road. Lastly, remember we drive on the left. Many a student, tired and content after their course, has left the car park driving as near to the starboard side of the road as is safe and practicable!

Summary

Emergencies are best avoided by proper preparation and regular maintenance. However, we advise you to practise emergency procedures on calm days so that you are prepared if the worst should happen at sea.

Questions

1 What is the procedure for bleeding an engine?
2 If you have an engine failure and have to manoeuvre on one engine, would you put the good engine next to the pontoon or on the outside?
3 What will you need to be able to offer someone a tow?
4 What precautions will you take in fog?
5 What precautions would you take if you had to stay at sea in rough weather?

Answers

1 Slacken the screw on the engine filter and operate the lift pump until fuel appears. Tighten the screw and slacken one of the injectors. Put a rag over the injector to protect your skin and eyes from pressurized fuel. Run the engine for a maximum of ten seconds on the starter. Fuel should have appeared on the rag; if it has, tighten the injector. Do the same with a second injector and the engine will probably start. Stop the engine immediately and tighten the injector.
2 When mooring with one engine, the good engine should be on the outside for optimum manoeuvrability.
3 If you are involved in towing, you will need to ensure that the towing vessel has enough power to pull the tow. You will also need a suitable length of line and a securing point on which to attach the tow line.
4 Take a fix, adjust your speed accordingly, hoist your radar reflector if it is not a permanent fixture, switch on your navigation lights and keep a good lookout and listening watch. Your crew should be in life-jackets and warm clothing. If you are in a busy shipping area, try to manoeuvre into shallow water and anchor if necessary. You should have white flares to hand, sound the appropriate fog signal and monitor your radar if you have one.
5 If you have to remain at sea, give yourself plenty of room. Stay away from shipping lanes, tidal races and shallow water. Make sure that all crew members are wearing life-jackets and harnesses if you think there is any risk of losing someone overboard. Stow all gear above and below decks. Ensure that all fixtures on deck are secure, for instance the dinghy or life-raft, and check that all hatches and locker lids are battened down. Take a fix before the visibility is reduced.

12

ELECTRONIC AIDS TO NAVIGATION

Coastal navigation operates on the principle of establishing your position relative to one or more points whose positions are known. As we have seen, measuring the bearing of your vessel from three known points identifiable on a chart gives a position fix. In open sea, however, there will not be physical objects to help determine your position, so some other system of measuring your range or bearing to fixed points must be employed. Although not strictly part of the Day Skipper syllabus, electronic navaids are becoming common in the leisure market, so have been included. In electronic navigation systems, man has generated fixed points on the earth, forming terrestrial navigation systems and in space, forming satellite navigation systems, whose positions are accurately known and from which the mariner or aviator can obtain a position. Transmissions emanate from these points, which can be intercepted by equipment onboard your vessel and allow you to deduce your range from that point. This is the basis of all electronic navigation systems.

Echo-Sounders

Echo sounders produce acoustic energy which is transmitted perpendicularly from a transducer to the seabed. Some of the transmitted energy is reflected back as an echo. By measuring the time delay between transmitted pulse and received echo, depth can be calculated. The display is commonly digital. It is worth remembering that there is a time delay involved and when travelling towards a steep mud bank at speed, you could well be aground before your echo sounder registers the fact that you are running out of water.

Incorrect scale selection can cause reading errors; for example, if the 100ft scale is selected and the depth is 120ft, the echo sounder will show 20ft. Disturbance due to turbulence under the transducer can cause false echoes. Mud or silt in the water can cause inaccurate returns.

Echo-sounders should be calibrated. Check the reading with a lead line on a firm flat bottom. This will enable any offset to be calculated due to the position of the transducer in the hull. Most modern echo-sounders allow an offset to be entered, either to enable depths to be measured from the keel, the lowest part of the hull, or the waterline. As mentioned before, make sure you know from which point the echo-sounder is measuring.

Logs

The impeller or paddle wheel type of log is usually hull mounted. The number of revolutions of the paddle wheel is proportional to the distance travelled through the water. Speed of rotation is proportional to the vessel's speed.

Most logs require some form of calibration exercise to be carried out before reliance can be placed on them. This usually takes the form of a series of runs up and down a measured mile. Speed is then calculated by measuring the time required to cover the mile. Averaged reciprocal runs should remove variations due to tidal stream. A correction factor can then be applied to the log to correct any error. See the maker's handbook for full details.

The log is fitted through the hull and it will be necessary to remove the paddle wheel from time to time, for example, if it becomes fouled by weed or tiny fish preventing it from working, or if your vessel is being lifted out of the water, to prevent the strops from damaging it. You should therefore either carry a special cap to replace it, or a soft wooden bung of appropriate size.

Radar

The radar set transmits a short pulse of microwave energy which, when it strikes an object, known as a target, is reflected back to the radar scanner. As the pulse travels at the speed of light, which is a constant, we can determine the range of the target by measuring the time interval between transmission and reception. In order to obtain a 360-degree scan, the aerial rotates. Every time an echo is received by the set, a spot is illuminated on the screen. Radar can only see in a direct line of sight. It cannot see through objects or over horizons. Measuring range with radar is very accurate, provided the target has a clear and well-defined front edge. Bearing is not so precise mainly due to the beamwidth of the aerial. Any two or more targets which enter the beam at the same time will appear as one target; reducing the gain can sometimes help.

Sea clutter is produced by echoes

If your vessel is being lifted, remove the log to prevent damage by the strops.

returning from nearby waves. The anti-sea clutter control decreases the receiver sensitivity at close range. This should have the effect of reducing weak random returns from waves while preserving returns from true targets. However, there is danger of losing weak nearby but legitimate targets. Rain and snow can return echoes giving a cotton-wool effect on the display. Reduce the gain and then switch in the anti-rain clutter control to produce a clearer picture.

Radar can be used as an aid to navigation and for collision avoidance. Range rings may be displayed on the screen. These rings, or better still, the variable range marker may be used to measure ranges from radar conspicuous objects and hence obtain a position fix as described in Chapter 8. Risk of collision exists if the projected track of any target on the screen cuts or passes near to the centre spot.

Racons are radar beacons situated on the coast, lightships or large buoys, which emit an identifiable signal when triggered by a radar. The response appears on your display as a line or broken line, with its nearest point being the location of the station.

The radar takes a relatively large amount of power, particularly when transmitting. Ensure batteries are not flattened by prolonged use without charging. Set the radar power switch to standby. Many modern radar sets have a fully automatic warm-up and auto-tune cycle. Once the initial picture has been established, set the range as required and adjust the brilliance.

Adjust the gain control until receiver noise speckle appears faintly on the screen. Choose a clear single echo and adjust the tune control for the best possible reception. If necessary, repeat the procedure. If appropriate, adjust anti-sea clutter or anti-rain clutter, but beware of reducing receiver sensitivity completely.

General Principle of Hyperbolic Navigation

Radio signals radiate from a group or chain of transmitters at the speed of light and can be detected by your navaid, giving a hyperbolic position line. As with conventional navigation, more than one line is required to establish your position. All radio navaids operating on the hyperbolic lattice principle suffer from the following accuracy problems:

Baseline Extension

Examination of the hyperbolic lattice structure in the baseline extension area shows that the hyperbolic position lines are becoming nearly parallel. This results in loss of precision in the fix. As far as possible, chains are arranged so that base line extension areas are over land where they are not a problem to the mariner (see Fig 51).

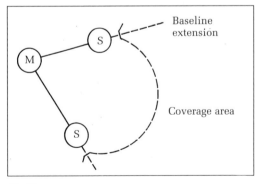

Fig 51.

Lane Separation

The further away from the transmitting stations, the wider are the lanes between position lines. Lanes are closest together along the baseline and therefore accuracy is highest here.

Changeover Areas

Receivers can become confused in the changeover area between adjacent chains. Manually choosing the chain you are heading towards can help.

Decca

The Decca system was one of the earliest hyperbolic position fixing systems and was developed for the Admiralty during the Second World War. However, Decca is now being superseded by GPS.

Loran-C

LORAN-C is a low frequency pulsed hyperbolic navigation system, operated by the US Coastguard. Responsibility is now being transferred to host nations and coverage is being extended to cover Northern Europe. Groundwave coverage is 800–1,200 nautical miles and up to 2,000 nautical miles using skywave. Accuracy is about 0.1 nautical mile in good groundwave coverage but may fall to more than 5 nautical miles using sky-wave. Chains consist of one master station, M, and up to four slave stations designated W, X, Y and Z. Two master/slave pairs are required to obtain a fix, e.g. M+W and M+X. Modern receivers with microprocessor control are capable

of displaying latitude and longitude as a direct read-out.

The best performance of the system is demonstrated when the repeatable accuracy is tested, using groundwave signals with good chain geometry. In practice, repeatable accuracy of 20–100 metres is regularly achieved. Two vessels both equipped with Loran-C can accurately rendezvous. As they approach each other, propagation paths become similar and any errors are the same for both vessels.

The Global Positioning System

NAVSTAR GPS: **NAV**igation **S**atellites with **T**ime **A**nd **R**anging. This is by far the most popular electronic navigation system available to date. GPS uses a constellation of twenty-one satellites plus three spares, orbiting at just over 20,000 kilometres above the earth. This provides at least four visible satellites from anywhere on the earth giving three-dimensional position fixing: latitude, longitude and altitude. GPS is based on measuring the user's range to three of these satellites. Each satellite transmits a message giving details of its position and enables the GPS receiver to calculate its range from the satellite.

Normal performance of the system was so good that the American Department of Defense, which controls the system, deliberately introduced errors into the transmitted information. This artificial degradation of accuracy is known as selective availability. Even when selective availability is switched on, accuracy should be within 150 metres.

Waypoint Navigation

A waypoint is a position, normally given in latitude and longitude, which can be stored in an electronic navigation aid's memory. It may be a point on an intended passage, or it may be a reference point from which the navaid will give a range and bearing.

When choosing waypoints, include one near the start of your passage to check the operation of your equipment. When including waypoints in an offshore passage, you can choose round figures to minimize risk of finger trouble. Waypoints should be entered on the boundaries of Traffic Separation Schemes and at the mid-point to advise of change of lane and therefore traffic direction. Choose a suitable waypoint for your landfall, not too close to your destination and preferably where you can confirm position by other means. If you choose a waypoint off a harbour entrance, put it on the leading line. You can also use waypoints to ensure safe distance off, when rounding headlands. Always keep a written list of your waypoints and their latitudes and longitudes.

Having entered the waypoints into your navaid's memory, they must be put into order to form a 'route' or 'sailplan'. Waypoints can be run in any order you desire, not necessarily numerically. Once the vessel is underway and heading for a waypoint, the navaid can provide a lot of useful data, such as speed or course made good, or speed or course over the ground. This information is calculated by the navaid by looking back at the vessel's progress, usually over the last four minutes. Tidal data can also be entered.

Useful functions for the Day Skipper include bearing and distance to next waypoint, which does not take account of tide or effects of leeway. If tidal information has been entered, then navaid will give course to steer to the next waypoint. Cross-track error gives the distance off the original track between waypoints that the vessel has drifted and usually a directing arrow to return to the track. Navaids will also display 'time to go' to the next waypoint and estimated time of arrival, which will be based on the present position and calculated speed made good over the last four minutes.

Summary

Electronic aids to navigation are becoming commonplace on motor boats of today. We have been flying by wire for many years now, but you will always find back-up systems on aeroplanes. This is the message we wish to convey. By all means use your GPS or whatever system you have, as an aid to navigation, but do not put your total trust in it. Remember any of these systems can be switched off and any piece of equipment can fail. The worst thing that can happen to your equipment in conventional navigation is that the lead in your pencil will break!

Questions

1 What information should you know about the reading from your echo-sounder?
2 How would you determine if risk of collision exists using radar?
3 Decca was one of the first hyperbolic fixing systems; what errors is it prone to?
4 Why was selective availability introduced to GPS?
5 What uses can be made of waypoints in electronic navigation aids?

Answers

1 It is important to know from which point the echo-sounder is reading. Depths can be measured from the keel, the lowest part of the hull, or the waterline.

2 Any target whose projected track on the screen cuts or passes near to the centre spot is on a collision course.

3 Baseline extension error occurs where the hyperbolic lines of position become nearly parallel. The further away from the transmitting stations, the wider are the lanes between position lines. In the change-over area between adjacent chains, receivers can become confused.

4 Normal performance of the system was so good, that selective availability was introduced deliberately to degrade accuracy.

5 When choosing waypoints include one near the start of your passage to check the operation of your equipment. Waypoints should be entered on the boundaries of Traffic Separation Schemes and at the mid-point to advise of change of lane and therefore traffic direction. Choose a suitable waypoint for your landfall, not too close to your destination and preferably where you can confirm position by other means. If you choose a waypoint off a harbour entrance, put it on the leading line. You can also use waypoints to ensure safe distance off, when rounding headlands.

INDEX